hassle **free**
gluten **free**

Jane Devonshire

*For my amazing Mum and Dad
and Mark, my wonderful husband.*

*Without you none of this could
have happened. You have supported
and loved me through both the hard
times and the very good times.*

Love you lots,
xxxx

hassle **free**
gluten **free**

Jane Devonshire

In association with Coeliac UK

with photography by
Mike Cooper

introduction

It's an incredible feeling to be sitting writing the introduction to my very own book, a book which is first and foremost about some of my favourite home recipes with treats and everyday food included. It also just happens to be gluten free because that's how I have cooked at home for the last 14 years since my youngest son, Ben, was diagnosed as a Coeliac aged two.

If you eat everything and anything, food is one of the most inclusive parts of our lives. It brings people together. Some of my very best moments in life have been sitting around a table sharing every type of food, from the most humble of dishes to the occasional Michelin starred meal. The simple joy of being able to order whatever I wanted from a menu or being included in a no fuss way in any party was something I have always taken for granted.

I was lucky that I have always had an absolute love of cooking, and to me food is just integral to my family. The word 'foodies' perfectly represents my family, as food is just one of our central and grounding cores. I truly believe that families that eat together stay together.

My father was a market trader and food salesman who brought home incredible produce from work. My mum was an amazing cook who could churn out wonderful food, often from very humble ingredients, so I grew up eating things like giblet stew and rabbit, as well as whatever was left behind or had caught dad's eye at market. This was in the days before the plethora of cookbooks, and access to huge numbers of recipes on the internet. Mum just has an intuitive understanding of food which I have taken on board, just by being in the kitchen and working with her and my nan. I am proud that I am not a fussy eater and that I have brought up my children to eat the same way.

However, Ben's diagnosis changed all of that. I began to appreciate how alienating it can be to not be able to partake in this most everyday of customs. Children's parties in particular were a minefield; pizza parties and fast food so often associated with children's activities became complicated. Ben had to learn to take a packed lunch with him and to be different, which is so hard when everyone is learning to fit in. Sometimes he didn't even get invited because obviously he couldn't go to a pizza-making party.

We were faced with the challenges of educating him – don't just eat any sweets at a party (honestly who would have thought Smarties have gluten in them!) – to teaching him to say no to adults who were adamant that what he was eating was OK. On one infamous occasion, one of our dearest family friends peeled the breadcrumbed skin from some fried chicken and told him it was fine to eat it. She was absolutely mortified by her mistake but it could so easily have been a nasty experience.

Food had become a minefield but I didn't want it to become the defining thing in Ben's life. For me, he had to learn to live with his diagnosis, understand it and get on with it. It was not an excuse to not be everything he wanted to be.

It became so important, therefore, that at home we ate gluten free. Yes Ben has a separate bread bin and toaster, and a separate cupboard for some of his food, but everyday meals were going to be inclusive. We were all going to eat the same.

So my challenge was to cook meals that my eldest children wouldn't moan about (a miracle in itself some days), and that Ben could eat. The last thing you want around a dinner table – which is fraught with all the normal traps that all parents encounter – was the refrain 'why do we have to eat this just because of Ben... I like real pizza or proper gravy...' The list was endless. My kids were great but they were kids, and who could blame them?

In all fairness, I could understand what they meant. Fourteen years ago, when Ben was first diagnosed, there was not a vast range of products available for people who needed to eat a gluten-free diet. Some of the food on offer, including basics like bread and pasta, was unpleasant to say the least. So I had to start from scratch at home, making recipes up, having total disasters, triumphs and genuinely discovering a way that I could daily feed my whole family a gluten-free diet.

We have had some real challenges, bread probably being the main one and cost another, but through necessity I persevered. It's now a constant joke in my house, but the question I ask most often is not do you like it, but 'can you tell it's gluten free?' The children are brutally honest and it has taken a while, but this is what I strive to achieve; to make food that people coming into my house are unaware is gluten free, but just think it is good food.

And why should Ben accept food of a lesser quality or taste? My answer: he shouldn't.

Being gluten free is not always a personal choice or preference. I am no food nutritionist and would never advocate any major changes in diet for most people. However, there are those who are genuinely intolerant to gluten as well as those that are diagnosed Coeliac.

I have found it so frustrating over the years to see Ben palmed off with food that is not fit for purpose, that is so sub-standard in flavour and texture. And sadly it happens in both restaurants and supermarkets. In addition, ready-made gluten-free food can be scarily expensive and, like a lot of ready-made food, it is full of additives and preservatives.

Of course I don't make everything for Ben, and he does have shop-bought treats. He loves ginger biscuits and I often buy them along with the occasional cake for a treat. Like any mum, I am not superhuman, and gluten-free fish fingers have been a favourite standby for a number of years, while the ability to buy the occasional pizza is a blessing when I am working away.

However day to day I cook, and I am lucky I love it. I am intrigued by it and want to persevere to get things right. It's my passion. Hence the MasterChef thing!

For years we have watched it as a family; I love it and admit to being a total addict. From Lloyd Grossman Sunday afternoons to watching the very first series featuring John Torode and Gregg Wallace, it's been a must-see programme in my house. For years the children had prompted me to enter, but I never thought I was good enough. This culminated in them taking matters into their own hands and filling in the form for me. Ben was instrumental in this and we did it one rainy summer's afternoon.

That silly afternoon has changed my life. I never believed I could win, I never believed I was good enough but I persevered and cooked what I loved and am still pinching myself that I have the trophy sitting on my mantelpiece. I loved my time on the show and it allowed me to experiment and push myself in a way I would never have achieved without it. It was a truly amazing experience and one I will always treasure.

There were ups and downs, not least the day I couldn't cook an egg(!), but I learnt so much and have gone on to make a career doing what I love; talking about and cooking food. The MasterChef experience taught me how creative I could be and how I could elevate my food to fine dining but truthfully my heart lies very much in family cookery, it's what I love and how I cook every day at home.

The recipes in this book are the product of fourteen years of cooking for my family each day and they represent just a small section of some of our favourite foods; I am constantly evolving these and thinking of new ways and flavour combinations. Some of the processes or 'my tips' will be different to traditional methods but I have found they work for me and my family day to day.

I also wanted this book to be, first and foremost, really accessible. All ingredients can be really easily sourced from your local supermarket or online. You don't need a cupboard full of different flours or obscure ingredients. In fact unless it's for taste I only use gluten-free plain flour with added raising agents or stabilisers; I find this helps me achieve results and takes a lot of the fuss out of baking in particular.

Where you source your flour from can make a huge difference to your cooking as well. Some flours have a bleached white and chalky texture and this will affect your results. I buy my flour online from Alevra. It is slightly more expensive but I find it gives me much better results.

I have had to adapt and completely change the way I do things and also accept that things will look different. Gluten-free baking in particular often involves quite a different approach, but there are some advantages.

For example, when making bread there is no knocking back, and once you have mastered the technique it's so easy to do. When it comes to baking, the final colour of your pastry or bread, as I talk about throughout the book, will be blonder than traditional non-gluten-free baking. Egg washing will help ensure more colour, but the temptation is often to overbake to achieve the deep golden colour we often associate with pastry in particular. Instead of relying on colour, you have to be a little more observant and notice if things look wet or greasy, and also, as with anything, the more you do it the more you become aware of what is right.

Cooking and eating should be about pleasure, not about stress, and I really hope the approach in this book helps you to cook delicious hassle-free, gluten-free food.

Jane x

hassle free, gluten free

a note on gluten cross-contamination

When you're maintaining a strict gluten-free diet you need to make sure you don't contaminate gluten-free food with any crumbs of food that contain gluten.

When you're cooking at home, whether for yourself or for your family and friends, here are some simple steps to follow that will help keep food preparation safe:

- Wash down surfaces before preparing food
- Cook gluten-free foods and foods that contain gluten in separate pans with separate utensils
- Standard washing up or using a dishwasher will remove gluten
- Washing up liquids are fine to use. There are very few that contain gluten, but if they do, standard rinsing will remove any traces
- You do not need to use separate cloths or sponges
- You may want to get separate bread boards to keep gluten-free and gluten-containing breads separate
- Use a separate toaster or toaster bags for gluten-free bread
- Use clean oil or a separate fryer for frying gluten-free foods
- Use different butter knives and jam spoons to prevent breadcrumbs from getting into condiments.

a note on ingredients

Where we know it is important that an ingredient is labelled gluten free, we have stated this in the recipe, such as ***gluten-free** flour*. For other ingredients which may not be labelled gluten free but which do not typically contain gluten we have put the symbol O against it, to remind you to double check the packaging to make sure gluten (wheat, barley, rye, oats) is not listed in the ingredients list.

nibbles, small dishes and lunches

Feta Cheese Mousse

makes about
500g

This is one of my go-to recipes. It works really well when served with the Roasted Beetroot with Pomegranate Molasses (page 112), or as a stand-alone dip; or you can use it as a base recipe and combine it with olives, tomatoes and basil for a really lovely twist.

1 x 200g pack feta cheese
1 x 250g pack cream cheese
125–150ml double cream
1 tablespoon lemon juice

Place the feta and cream cheese in a food processor and blend until smooth. Alternatively, use a stick blender.

With the processor still running, add the cream until you have a thick, smooth, mousse-like texture. Add lemon juice to taste, and serve.

Cheese Straws

makes between
6 and 8

These resemble breadsticks, and I put them out as snacks for adults and kids ... if they make it past the cooling tray.

125g **gluten-free** *plain flour*
½ teaspoon smoked paprika
½ teaspoon xanthan gum
75g unsalted butter
85g mature Cheddar cheese, grated
1 large egg yolk
25g Parmesan, finely grated
sea salt and freshly ground
  black pepper

You will need
a silicone baking mat or lightly oiled
  baking tray

Preheat the oven to 200°C/180°C Fan/Gas Mark 6.

Sift the flour, smoked paprika, xanthan gum and a pinch of salt into a bowl or food processor. Add the butter and rub between your fingertips or process until you have fine breadcrumbs. If using a food processor, transfer the crumbs to a bowl.

My Tip
Instead of the smoked paprika suggested here, you can use many different flavourings in these straws, including onion seeds, dry mustard seeds, fennel seeds or coriander seeds.

Add the Cheddar cheese and egg yolk and stir to form a dough. If necessary, add 2–3 tablespoons of water, a little at a time, until a stiff dough is achieved.

Take a ball of dough, the diameter of a 10-pence piece, and roll out into a thin breadstick-like shape. Repeat with the remaining dough.

Scatter the Parmesan and a little sea salt and pepper on to your work surface, and gently roll the cheese sticks in the mixture to coat the outside.

Transfer to the baking mat or tray and bake in the oven for 15–20 minutes, until golden. Leave to cool, then serve.

Fried Chorizo and Halloumi Nibbles

serves 4–6

This recipe is so easy and packed with flavour. I fry it up just as people arrive and serve it with cocktail sticks as an appetiser. I also serve it with Focaccia (page 181), as people love to dip it into the spicy oil.

1 x chorizo ring (approx. 200–240g), chopped into chunks
olive oil
1 x 225g pack halloumi cheese, chopped into chunks

Fry the chorizo gently in a little olive oil until starting to crisp, then remove from the oil and set aside in a bowl.

Gently fry the halloumi in the chorizo oil until golden and cooked through; it will have a lovely puffy texture. Remove from the oil and combine with the chorizo.

Serve the fried chorizo and halloumi chunks in a bowl with cocktail sticks on the side so people can help themselves.

My Tip
The oil that comes out of the chorizo is wonderful, but it does stain so napkins and cocktail sticks are a must.

Spiced Almonds

serves 4–6

Addictive little nibbles, which are so easy to prepare and lovely served with drinks or just to snack on for movie night.

200g whole almonds, skin on
1 tablespoon olive oil
½ tablespoon sea salt
○ *½ tablespoon ras el hanout*
½ teaspoon hot chilli powder

Place all the ingredients in a frying pan over a low heat and stir to combine.

Keep stirring until the spices just start smoking and all the almonds are coated evenly in the mixture; take care not to burn the spices.

Remove from the heat, place the nuts in a bowl and serve.

Chickpea, Spinach and **Basil Dip**

makes about
450g

Quick, easy and tasty, this dip is perfect with crudités, or served as a dollop on the side of barbecued meats. I like to combine it with cooked cooled new potatoes for a different style of potato salad.

1 x 400g can of chickpeas, drained and rinsed
150g baby spinach
1 garlic clove
25g fresh basil
1 red chilli (optional); I use a milder chilli and remove the seeds, but leave the seeds in if you like it hot
100–150ml olive oil, plus extra for drizzling
juice of 1½ lemons
sea salt

Place the chickpeas, spinach, garlic, basil and chilli, if using, in a food processor, or in a jug with a stick blender, and blend, adding the olive oil gradually until you reach a smooth consistency.

Add lemon juice and salt to taste, then serve immediately, drizzled with a little more olive oil.

Variation
Make potato salad by combining 450g cooked cooled new potatoes with the dip. Garnish with fresh basil and serve with a drizzle of olive oil. This would serve 4–6 people.

hassle free, gluten free

Carrot and **Parsnip Hummus** with **Rose Harissa** and **Heritage Carrots**

Serves 4 as a starter
(more if serving as a
sharing platter)

I use heritage carrots here for colour contrast, as they look so pretty on the plate. The hummus makes a lovely starter dish with the heritage carrots, served with Focaccia (page 181), and any leftovers can be served on their own as a dip or in wraps and sandwiches. I love rose harissa, but ordinary harissa paste can be used instead.

1 tablespoon cumin seeds
1 tablespoon coriander seeds
4 large (orange) carrots
2 parsnips
2 garlic cloves
½ teaspoon crushed chilli
12 baby mixed heritage carrots (if you can only find larger ones, they should be chopped into batons)
50g butter
***gluten-free** vegetable stock*
2 tablespoons rose harissa paste (add a little more if you like it spicy)
3 tablespoons extra virgin olive oil
2 tablespoons lemon juice, to taste
1 x 400g can of chickpeas
sea salt

Roast the cumin and coriander seeds gently in a frying pan for a couple of minutes, until you can smell the spices and they start to pop; agitate the pan while frying to stop the seeds burning, which will make the spices bitter. Remove from the heat and use a pestle and mortar to grind to a fine powder.

Peel and dice the regular carrots and parsnips and place in a pan with the garlic cloves and crushed chilli. Cover with salted water, bring to the boil and cook until tender, about 8 minutes depending on the size of the dice.

Carefully wash and scrub the heritage carrots clean, then trim the tops. Place in a pan with the butter, enough stock to cover, 1 tablespoon of rose harissa and a little salt, bring to the boil and cook until al dente, about 5 minutes depending on the size of the carrots. Don't overcook the carrots as they need some texture.

While the carrots are cooking, make the dressing. Combine the remaining rose harissa with the olive oil, 1 tablespoon of lemon juice and a little salt in a bowl. Once the heritage carrots are cooked, drain and coat with the harissa dressing and set aside.

Drain the regular carrots and parsnips, reserving some of the water. Transfer them to a food processor and blend until smooth, then add the remaining lemon juice, a little of the coriander and cumin powder, and salt to taste, and blend again. Add the drained chickpeas and blend again, but leave some texture this time. You may need to add a little of the reserved water to the mixture to loosen it a little.

To serve, put a big spoonful of hummus on each plate, dress with the carrots and harissa dressing, and lightly sprinkle with coriander and cumin seed powder.

Sweet Pickled Vegetables

serves 4–6
as part of a
sharing platter

I like to serve pickled vegetables with many dishes as they can really lift a meal. This is a very simple pickle using rice wine vinegar, which is softer than many other vinegars. Please feel free to experiment with different vinegars and aromatics. Chilli, bay leaves and lots of other flavours can be added to this basic pickle recipe to add more flavour.

250ml rice wine vinegar
250g caster sugar
2–3 black peppercorns
2 carrots, cut into batons or your
   desired shape
2 banana shallots, cut into thin rings
200g radishes, sliced thinly

Place the rice wine vinegar, sugar, peppercorns and 500ml of water into a saucepan and bring to the boil for a few minutes, then remove from the heat and remove the peppercorns.

Place the vegetables into three separate jars and just cover them with the pickling liquor. The thicker the vegetable, the longer it will take to pickle: when thinly sliced they can take 5–7 minutes; if using whole or thicker slices, I would leave them for up to an hour.

My Tip
You can experiment with any of your favourite vegetables, from mushrooms to beetroots, so use whatever takes your fancy.

hassle free, gluten free

Pickled Apple
with **Rosemary**

To me, getting the centrepiece dish of a meal right is key – a beautifully cooked piece of fish, meat or vegetable is a must, but what elevates that plate to something truly special are the little additional touches that chefs, and indeed you, add to your food. Throughout the book I have tried to outline a few of the tips and tricks I have picked up along the way. Making your own stocks and sauces, purées and pickles adds so much to a dish. This particular pickle is great served with pork or pheasant.

100ml rice wine vinegar
splash of white wine vinegar
100g caster sugar
at least 6 large sprigs of
* fresh rosemary*
3 English Braeburn apples

Place all the ingredients except the apples into a pan with 200ml of water and bring to the boil. Bruise the rosemary with a wooden spoon to get as much flavour as possible out of it. Once you are happy with the strength of the pickling liquid and the flavour of the rosemary is coming through, remove it from the heat.

I like to use a melon baller or the teaspoon of my measuring spoons to cut out semi-circles of the apple, including the skin. Put the pieces of apple into the pickling liquid immediately. Leave for at least 15 minutes, or until you are happy with the flavour of the apple. I use this pickle within a few hours of making it, otherwise the apples lose their texture and become soft.

Clockwise, from top left: sweet pickled vegetables (page 22); carrot and parsnip hummus with rose harissa and heritage carrots (page 21); flat bread (page 190); Mediterranean tempura vegetables with spicy tomato dip (page 28); smoked trout scotch egg (page 27); and watercress pesto (page 26)

Watercress Pesto

makes 350g

I live near the best watercress beds in the world in Alresford in Hampshire, so I have access to the most amazing fresh watercress you can imagine. I am lucky we all love it, as I use it in many different ways, almost like a herb. This pesto goes well with many things, but is exceptionally good with trout; it's such a natural synergy as they both thrive in the same chalk streams.

200g watercress
250ml rapeseed oil or flavourless
*   vegetable oil*
50g blanched hazelnuts
1–2 tablespoons lemon juice
sea salt

Add the watercress into boiling water and leave for 2–3 minutes, then drain and plunge into a bowl of iced water to cool. Drain again and squeeze out any excess water.

Place the watercress in a blender with the oil, blanched hazelnuts and 1 tablespoon of lemon juice, and blend to a smooth purée; you may need to add more oil.

Add more lemon juice to taste, if desired, and maybe a little salt, depending on the saltiness of the accompanying dishes.

hassle free, gluten free

Smoked Trout
Scotch Egg

serves 4

These are really yummy and a lighter version of the traditional Scotch egg. I use smoked trout as I live very close to the River Test and trout is easily sourced. Good smoked salmon will work equally well.

6 quail's eggs (you only need 4, but better to have extra just in case)
white wine vinegar, to cover the eggs
2 banana shallots, finely chopped
25g butter
200g cold-smoked trout or good smoked salmon
1 teaspoon lemon juice
○ *150g polenta*
*100g **gluten-free** plain flour*
2 eggs
black pepper

Add the quail's eggs into boiling water for exactly 2 minutes 15 seconds. Remove the eggs and plunge into iced water to cool.

Cover the cooled eggs with white wine vinegar and leave for about 10–15 minutes. The speckles will disappear and the vinegar will froth up, but don't worry; this process makes it so much easier to peel them. Peel the eggs carefully and set aside.

Sauté the banana shallots in the butter for 5 minutes with a good grind of black pepper, until the shallots are soft and translucent, then remove from the heat and leave to cool.

Place the cooled shallots and smoked fish in a blender and pulse until a mince-like texture. Add lemon and pepper to taste.

Take one quail's egg and one heaped dessertspoon of smoked trout mixture (about 50g). Gently press the smoked fish mixture into the palm of your hand to make a circle, then carefully encase the egg and roll it into a ball; this is quite a delicate process so take your time. Refrigerate for about 1 hour until firm.

Place the polenta in a shallow bowl, the flour in a second bowl, and beat the eggs in a third bowl.

Place the Scotch eggs first into the flour, then into the egg, and then into the polenta, ensuring each one is evenly coated. When all are coated, you can return to the fridge for up to 24 hours, covered, or cook immediately.

When the eggs are needed, fill a heavy-based pan one-third full with oil and heat to a temperature of 180°C. If you don't have a thermometer, simply drop a cube of bread into the pan; if it sinks then rises, bubbling gently, your oil is hot enough. Alternatively, use a deep fat fryer.

Fry off the eggs until the outer crumb is golden brown. These can be eaten cold, but I think they are best served warm.

Mediterranean Tempura Vegetables with Spicy Tomato Dip

28

serves 4 as a starter
(or more as part of
a sharing platter)

A great sharing platter, which uses store-cupboard ingredients to make a spicy dip. I tend to put a big bowl of this out and serve a group of guests.

1 courgette, chopped into batons
1 red pepper, chopped into batons
1 yellow pepper, chopped into batons
75g pitted black olives from a jar
sunflower oil

For the tempura batter
125g rice flour, plus extra for tossing
   the vegetables
125g cornflour
10g chopped fresh basil
1 large egg
a good grind of black pepper
250ml ice-cold club soda

For the dip
75g roasted red peppers from a jar
25g red jalapeños from a jar
50g pitted black olives from a jar
50g tomato passata
25ml brine from the olive jar

Combine all the dip ingredients and blitz using a stick blender, then set aside.

Dust the vegetables lightly in rice flour – they can all be combined as they have the same cooking time.

Line a large bowl or tray with kitchen towel and have a slotted spoon ready.

Fill a heavy-based pan one-third full of sunflower oil and heat to 180°C. If you don't have a thermometer, simply drop a little of the batter into the pan – if it sinks then rises, sizzling, your oil is hot enough. Alternatively, use a deep fat fryer.

For the batter, place the flours, basil, egg and pepper in a bowl but don't mix. Add the ice-cold club soda and whisk quickly. Immediately add a handful of the vegetables to the batter to coat them, then fry them off quickly, for about 2 minutes – the batter does not go golden but crisps quickly.

Remove from the oil with the slotted spoon and place on the kitchen towel, then repeat the process until all the vegetables are cooked. Make sure the oil stays at the correct temperature: if you put too many vegetables into the pan, the temperature will drop and the tempura can become oily.

Serve immediately with the dip alongside.

hassle free, gluten free

Smoked Salmon and **Peppered Cream Cheese Tart**

serves 4

As busy people I think we all need a few shortcuts sometimes, so this is a cheat's tart, using the flavoured cream cheese readily available from any supermarket. And if you want to miss the pastry stage altogether, it can be made in greased silicone moulds.

1 x quantity Shortcrust Pastry (page 194)
1 x 150g pack black pepper cream cheese
100ml double cream
4 eggs
200g smoked salmon, roughly chopped

You will need
a 20cm round x 4cm deep loose-bottomed tin and baking beans

Preheat the oven to 200°C/180°C Fan/Gas Mark 6.

Gluten-free pastry is quite hard to work with, so I find it easier to roll out the pastry, then cut out the base, using the tin as a template. Put the pastry base in place, then cut out the sides, placing them gently around the tin. Work around the base, using your fingers to ensure a seal is made between base and sides, then trim the top edge with a knife.

Line the pastry case with baking parchment, fill with baking beans and blind bake for 18–20 minutes, until the pastry is crispy but not coloured. Remove from the oven and carefully remove the baking beans and paper, but leave the oven on.

In a large bowl, combine the cream cheese, cream and 3 of the eggs with an electric whisk or wooden spoon until there are no lumps.

Transfer the cream cheese mixture into the pastry case and add the chopped smoked salmon, distributing it equally over the mixture.

Beat the remaining egg and use it to egg wash the top of the tart sides. (This is optional but will help the pastry turn a little golden.)

Place the tart in the oven and cook for 25 minutes, until the top is raised and golden. Do note that gluten-free pastry can be less golden than non-gluten-free pastry, so do not be tempted to overcook.

My Tip
The tart can be eaten warm or cold. You can also use the garlic and herb version of the cream cheese for an equally lovely result.

Asparagus and Bacon Tart

serves 4

I like to add the blue cheese to this tart, but my husband hates it, so it's entirely optional. The tart is lovely served warm, but is great eaten cold as a picnic dish, too.

1 x quantity of Cheese Shortcrust
Pastry (page 194)
200g smoked bacon, chopped
knob of butter
125g thin asparagus spears, cut into
1cm lengths
3 large eggs
175ml double cream
a good grind of black pepper
30g soft blue cheese (optional); I use
Saint Agur

You will need

a 20cm round x 4cm deep loose-
bottomed tin and baking beans

Preheat the oven to 200°C/180°C Fan/Gas Mark 6.

Line the tin with the cheese pastry. Gluten-free pastry is quite hard to work with, so I find it easier to roll out the pastry, then cut out the base, using the tin as a template. Put the pastry base in place, then cut out the sides, placing them gently around the tin. Work around the base, using your fingers to ensure a seal is made between base and sides, then trim the top edge with a knife.

Line the pastry base with baking parchment, fill with baking beans, and blind bake for 20 minutes, until the pastry is crisp but not coloured. Remove from the oven and carefully remove the baking beans and paper, but leave the oven on.

Fry the bacon in a little butter until golden and crispy, then remove onto a plate. Add the chopped asparagus spears to the bacon fat and cook for 2 minutes, then transfer to the plate with the bacon.

Combine 2 of the eggs, cream and pepper in a large bowl.

Put the bacon and asparagus in the base of the blind-baked pastry case and crumble the blue cheese over the top, if using. Pour over the cream and egg mixture evenly, so it covers all the asparagus and bacon.

Beat the remaining egg and use it to egg wash the exposed edges of the pastry. This is optional but it will help the pastry take on some colour, although it will never take on the golden colour of non-gluten free pastry.

Transfer to the oven and cook for 20–25 minutes, or until the tart has no wobble.

Avocado Bhaajis

makes 12

A fun and spicy way to eat avocado, this is a great dish for vegetarians, as well as something a little different. As always, if you like things a little spicier, feel free to up the chilli content.

2 tablespoons natural yogurt

*4 tablespoons **gluten-free** gram flour*

½ teaspoon very finely chopped red chilli, plus extra to garnish (I remove the seeds, but leave them in if you like it hot)

½ tablespoon lime juice

1 teaspoon sea salt

2 medium ripe avocados

sunflower oil, for frying

chopped fresh coriander, to garnish

lime wedges, to garnish

In a bowl or jug, combine the yogurt, gram flour, chilli, lime juice, salt and 2–3 tablespoons of water to make a thick batter.

Cut the avocado into 1cm cubes and combine immediately into the batter.

Fill a heavy-based pan one-third full with oil and heat to a temperature of 180°C. If you don't have a thermometer, simply drop a little of the batter into the pan; if it sinks then rises, sizzling, your oil is hot enough. Alternatively, use a deep fat fryer.

Take a dessertspoonful of the batter and avocado mixture and drip it carefully into the hot oil. Fry until golden on all sides. I do this in batches, as if you overload the pan the temperature of the oil will drop and you won't get golden, crispy bhajis. Set each one aside on kitchen towel as you go.

Once all the bhaajis are cooked, pile onto a plate straight away and garnish with chilli, chopped coriander and lime wedges.

My Tip
You can swap the coriander for flat-leaf parsley, if you prefer.

Prawn Bhaajis with **Coriander** Dipping Sauce

serves 4

I love prawns, and if they are on a menu I will always order them. This version in a spicy curried batter with coriander dip is a real crowd pleaser. When I make these, Harry tries to devour the whole plate, so they are definitely one of his favourites.

2 teaspoons garam masala
2 teaspoons ground turmeric
2 teaspoons ground cumin
¼ teaspoon chilli powder
*4 tablespoons **gluten-free** gram flour*
1 teaspoon sea salt
4 teaspoons lemon juice
12 raw king prawns, unpeeled (or 1 x 180g pack of raw king prawns)
sunflower oil, for deep frying

For the coriander dipping sauce
100g fresh coriander, leaves picked and stalks discarded
2 tablespoons natural yogurt
1 red chilli: ½ with seeds removed, ½ finely chopped
1 teaspoon lemon juice
pinch of sea salt, to taste

For the dipping sauce, blanch three-quarters of the coriander leaves in boiling water for 30–40 seconds. Drain, then place in a jug with the yoghurt and ½ chilli with the seeds removed, and use a stick blender to blend to a smooth sauce. Add the lemon juice and salt to taste. Transfer to a bowl and garnish with the chopped chilli and remaining coriander leaves.

Place the garam masala, turmeric, cumin, chilli powder, gram flour, salt and lemon juice into a bowl with 2 tablespoons of water and stir to make a thick paste; it should be a coating consistency, so add a little more water if needed.

Using a sharp knife, cut along the dark seam line and remove the vein from each of the prawns. Add the prawns to the batter and stir gently, making sure that all are evenly coated.

Fill a heavy-based pan one-third full with oil and heat to a temperature of 180°C. If you don't have a thermometer, simply drop a little of the batter into the pan; if it sinks then rises, sizzling, your oil is hot enough. Alternatively, use a deep fat fryer.

While the oil is heating, prepare a bowl or plate covered in kitchen towel. Once the oil is ready, add the prawns individually to the pan until the batter on the bhaji is a deep golden colour, then remove from the oil and place on kitchen towel to drain.

Repeat the process until all the prawns are cooked, and serve immediately with the coriander dipping sauce.

Left: prawn bhaajis (page 33)
Right: avocado bhaajis (page 32)

Croque Monsieur Croquettes

serves 4–6

I love a croque monsieur – it's my favourite toastie (probably because it's the most fattening!). This dish is reminiscent of those flavours, and great to prepare in advance and have on standby for a brunch/lunch, especially if you have been on a long dog walk or standing on the sidelines of a rugby pitch on a cold morning. These can be shallow fried or baked – the choice is yours.

400g cold mashed potato
250g diced cold ham or ham hock (smoked or unsmoked)
○ 2 tablespoons mayonnaise
100g grated mature Cheddar
150g (drained weight) ball of mozzarella, finely chopped
○ 2 tablespoons wholegrain mustard
4 large eggs
100g **gluten-free** plain flour
○ 120g fine polenta
sunflower oil (if frying)
sea salt

Put the potato, ham, mayonnaise, Cheddar, mozzarella, mustard, 1 egg and a little salt into a large bowl and stir to combine thoroughly. Shape the mixture into about ten hamburger-sized patties and place on a lightly floured baking tray. Transfer to the fridge for 30 minutes to chill.

Put the flour in a shallow bowl. Beat the remaining 3 eggs and place these in a separate bowl, then put the polenta into a third bowl.

Dip each patty into the flour, then the egg, then the polenta to coat evenly. You can refrigerate them overnight if preparing in advance, or use immediately.

Preheat the oven to 200°C/180°C Fan/Gas Mark 6 and cook for 40 minutes, turning halfway through; alternatively, fry the patties slowly in a little sunflower oil until heated all the way through and golden brown, about 2–3 minutes. They will be crispier if fried.

My Tip
There is a tendency of gluten-free food to look paler than perhaps you would expect, so as long as the croquettes are heated all the way through they will be cooked.

These are great served with a salad or with poached eggs.

The **Best Garlic Mushrooms**

serves 4–6
as a side

I use this recipe as a base for soup (just add some cream and gluten-free stock); on toasted focaccia for crostini-type starters; and with a poached duck egg and bacon-wrapped asparagus for a brunch starter dish. The dish is easy to prepare and very versatile.

300g large flat mushrooms, chopped
1 x 250g pack white mushrooms
large sprig of fresh thyme,
  leaves picked
large knob of unsalted butter
1 tablespoon olive oil
2 garlic cloves, minced
sea salt and freshly ground black
  pepper, to taste

Place all the ingredients in a frying pan and sauté gently for 10–12 minutes, until juicy and cooked through. Season to taste. These can be prepared in advance and warmed up when needed.

Mini Savoury Doughnuts with **Cheese**

makes about 30

We all love doughnuts, yet for ages I couldn't get the recipe right. These lovely little light savoury doughnuts can be served as a little pre-appetiser or just as a snack. They are best eaten straight away, but you can make them in the morning and then reheat for 5 minutes when you need them. I have to say a huge thank you to my great friend Juanita Hennessey, whose recipe I have adapted to gluten-free.

100g unsalted butter
1 teaspoon golden caster sugar
150g **gluten-free** plain flour
1 teaspoon xanthan gum
100g grated Parmesan, plus 25g
   to serve
4 large eggs, beaten
sunflower oil, for frying
sea salt

Put the butter, 300ml water and sugar into a large saucepan and bring to the boil, making sure all the butter has melted. Once boiling, turn the heat down to a simmer.

Sift the flour, xanthan gum and a pinch of salt into a bowl, then add to the water and butter mixture. Beat well with a wooden spoon until you have a ball of smooth paste; this will go lumpy to begin with but do persevere.

Remove from the heat and place on a steady surface.

Add the Parmesan and mix in. Slowly add the egg in 5–6 batches. I use an electric whisk, but your wooden spoon and muscles will do the work too. After you have added a little egg, beat or whisk until all of it is incorporated. If using an electric whisk, the mixture will creep up the whisks – just use a spoon and push it back down. Once all the egg is incorporated you will have a smooth, sticky, thick batter.

Fill a heavy-based pan one-third full with oil and heat to a temperature of 180°C. If you don't have a thermometer, simply drop a little of the batter into the pan; if it sinks then rises, sizzling, your oil is hot enough. Alternatively, use a deep fat fryer.

Drop a small spoonful of the mixture into the oil. Don't overload the pan or the temperature of the oil will drop – I cook them in batches of six. Fry for 5–6 minutes, turning halfway to get an even golden colour.

Remove the doughnuts from the oil using a slotted spoon and shake off any excess oil. Place on kitchen towel and repeat the process until all the mixture has been used. Just before serving, sprinkle over the remaining Parmesan.

Lamb Shank Soup

serves 6
for lunch or
4 for dinner

Lamb shanks used to be so cheap that they made a very economical meal. That's not the case now, sadly, however one lamb shank goes a long way, and this dish can be thrown in a pot and just left to do its own thing while you get on with life.

1 x 400g lamb shank
4 large carrots, chopped
1 onion, chopped
1 leek, chopped
200g chopped swede
2 stalks celery (include leaves and
    hearts if you have them), chopped
1 litre **gluten-free** lamb stock
2 bay leaves
2–3 thyme sprigs, leaves picked
pinch of sea salt and a good grinding
    of black pepper

Put all the ingredients into a saucepan; try to use a pan that is not too big so that the stock covers the lamb shank.

Simmer over a low heat for about 1 hour, until the meat is completely tender and falling off the bone. Remove the lamb shank and discard the bay leaves.

Using two forks, shred the meat off the bone. Return the meat to the pan and, using a stick blender, combine to create a thick soup. Adjust the seasoning to taste – we like ours peppery – and serve.

hassle free, gluten free

Chicken and Sweetcorn Soup

serves 4–6

Inspired by Chinese chicken and sweetcorn soup, there is something so warming and comforting about this soup that when I have a cold or am feeling a bit under the weather, I always find myself making a pot. It is a very quick soup to put together – just what is needed when you want something easy. If you decide to use chicken breasts instead of thighs, be very careful with the poaching; even though we have velveted the chicken, it can dry out quickly.

2 large eggs, separated
2 tablespoons cornflour
400g boneless, skinless
  chicken thighs, chopped into
  bite-sized pieces
*2 tablespoons **gluten-free** soy sauce*
1 small red chilli, finely chopped
2.5cm piece of fresh ginger, grated
  (or ½ teaspoon ground ginger)
1 garlic clove, finely chopped
splash of sunflower oil
*500ml **gluten-free** chicken stock*
1 x 410g can of creamed sweetcorn
1 x 195g can of sweetcorn in
  water, drained
○ *splash of chilli sauce or Sriracha*
  sauce (optional)

Put the egg whites and cornflour in a large bowl and beat together until no lumps remain. Add the diced chicken and soy sauce, and stir to ensure the chicken is evenly coated. Set aside for 15 minutes.

Place the chilli, ginger and garlic in a non-stick saucepan with a splash of oil and gently cook through for about a minute, until the garlic is softened, stirring all the time to ensure it does not burn. Add the chicken stock, stir and bring to the boil, then reduce the heat to a simmer.

Add the chicken thigh pieces and stir in rapidly, then leave to simmer to gently poach the chicken. Depending on thickness this will take no more than 5 minutes. Remember the chicken will be very soft as it has been velveted, so it's best to take a piece out and cut it open to check it's cooked.

Add both cans of corn and stir to combine.

Whisk the egg yolks and pour into the soup, stirring to combine, then add the chilli sauce, if using – I love chilli, so will always add a splash of sauce to mine.

My Tip
This is a great way to use up cold leftover roast chicken. Shred the cooked chicken into the soup once all the other ingredients are cooked and heat through. It won't have quite the same depth of flavour as the chicken hasn't been marinated or cooked in the soup, but it will still taste wonderful.

Minestrone Soup

serves 6

I love serving soup, especially when the kids came home from school, as it stopped them snacking on rubbish until the dinner was ready. I have adapted classic recipes to my family's tastes – this soup is packed full of vegetables, and I use canned pulses instead of pasta to add substance.

splash of olive oil
200g chopped pancetta or
*   smoked bacon*
1 leek, chopped
1 large onion, chopped
3 garlic cloves, finely chopped
3–4 sticks celery, chopped
*   (approx. 150g)*
4–5 carrots, chopped
*   (approx. 150g)*
1 chilli (optional)
2 tablespoons dried mixed herbs
1 litre passata
*1 litre **gluten-free** chicken stock*
3 large kale leaves, stalks removed
1 x 400g can cannellini
*   beans, drained*
1 x 400g can green/puy
*   lentils, drained*
freshly grated Parmesan, to serve
sea salt and freshly ground
*   black pepper*

Heat the olive oil in a large stock pot with the chopped pancetta, leek, onion and garlic, and sauté gently until translucent.

Add the celery, carrots, chilli and dried herbs and sauté for another 5 minutes.

Add the passata and chicken stock and cook for a further 5 minutes, then add the kale, beans and lentils and simmer for 7–8 minutes, until the vegetables are just cooked.

Season with salt and pepper to taste, and serve with a really generous grating of fresh Parmesan.

My Tip
I always have a stockpile of different types of canned beans and pulses in my store-cupboard. I use them in minestrone soup instead of pasta and I think it's an improvement. The pasta in the original version can go soggy, whereas with beans the soup can be eaten over a couple of days if kept refrigerated. Beans can also be added quickly to stews and curries to bulk out the ingredients and make them go further if you suddenly get more people for dinner – and the bonus is that they are a healthy addition.

Spanish Omelette

Whenever I cook new potatoes I always boil twice what I need and keep the rest in the fridge, ready to fry them up for breakfast, make a potato salad, throw them around a chicken while it's roasting, or make my favourite classic Spanish omelette. This is one of my go-to dishes, served hot or cold with a simple tomato salad for lunch, or cut into squares for a tapas-style starter.

275g cold cooked new potatoes, cut into bite-sized chunks
1 medium onion, diced
2 tablespoons dried mixed herbs
25g butter
3 tablespoons olive oil
6 large eggs
3 tablespoons milk
sea salt

You will need
a 28cm non-stick frying pan

Put the potatoes, onion, herbs, butter, oil and a good pinch of salt into your frying pan and fry gently over a low heat. You are trying to get the flavours to infuse into the potato, so don't rush this process; keep frying and stirring occasionally until everything starts to turn a lovely golden brown, about 5 minutes, then remove from the heat. You can leave the ingredients at this stage for a good few hours, as the flavours will just develop, then finish off the omelette before your guests arrive.

Whisk the eggs and milk in a bowl. Reheat the potato and onion if necessary, then add the eggs and milk to the frying pan. Use a fish slice to move the mixture about – it will look scrambled until it starts to come together. Make sure the filling is evenly distributed and continue to cook over a low heat. When you can see the egg start to come away from the sides of the pan, or when the base of the omelette is golden brown (use a blunt knife to gently lift it), remove from the heat.

Place the frying pan under a hot grill for a minute or two to ensure the top of the omelette is cooked. Alternatively, cover the frying pan with foil or a lid while the omelette is still cooking, to ensure the egg is cooked all the way through.

Once cooked, turn it out onto a large plate (I use a pizza stone) and slice as required.

dinner, supper and food for guests

Vegetable Curry

serves 4–6

This is a lovely side dish, but also great as a midweek meal when trying to not eat meat every day. It is so much easier to make the curry paste in a food processor or using a hand blender.

500ml **gluten-free** *vegetable stock*
1 large stalk of lemongrass, bashed
150g cauliflower, cut into
 small florets
150g broccoli, cut into small florets
150g diced carrot
1 teaspoon sea salt
1–2 teaspoons fresh lime juice
25g chopped fresh coriander leaves

For the curry paste
25g ginger root, grated
25g turmeric root, grated
 (if available), or 1 teaspoon
 ground turmeric
1 onion, finely chopped
3–4 garlic cloves, finely grated
40g very finely chopped fresh
 coriander (stalks and leaves)
2 tablespoons sunflower oil

For the curry paste, place all the ingredients into a blender with 50ml water and blitz.

Put the paste into a non-stick pan and cook down slowly for around 15 minutes, until the garlic and onion are cooked and a stiff paste is achieved. You will need to stir continuously to ensure nothing burns, as no browning should occur. This is a slow process and if the paste is not cooked down properly, the curry will be bitter.

Add the vegetable stock to the curry paste and stir in well. Add the bashed lemongrass stalk, cauliflower, broccoli, carrot and salt, stir, and leave to simmer for about 8 minutes, until the vegetables are cooked but still retain their firmness. Do not cover with a lid.

If the curry is a little wet once the vegetables are cooked, turn up the heat to reduce the sauce but be careful not to overcook the vegetables. Remove from the heat and discard the lemongrass. Add lime juice to taste, stir through the chopped coriander leaves, and serve.

Mushroom Risotto

serves 4 as a
main course, or
6 as a side dish
or starter

This risotto is brimming with flavour and very rich.
It's a wonderful vegetarian dish if you use vegetable
stock, although I prefer beef stock for extra flavour.
Preparing a risotto is a labour of love and takes time.
It's the perfect dish to make if you are in the kitchen
chatting to friends with a nice glass of wine, as you
cook everything slowly, from sautéing the shallots to
adding the stock. It is not a dish to put on the hob and
leave – you need to be hovering around.

25g mixed dried mushrooms
1 litre **gluten-free** beef or
  vegetable stock
4 banana shallots, finely chopped
5g picked fresh thyme leaves
50g butter
olive oil
4–5 garlic cloves, finely chopped
100g chestnut mushrooms, chopped
200g large, flat field
  mushrooms, chopped
225g risotto rice
50g grated Parmesan
30g cream cheese
good handful of fresh flat-leaf
  parsley, roughly chopped
1 tablespoon good balsamic
  vinegar (optional)
sea salt and freshly ground
  black pepper

Put the dried mushrooms and stock into a saucepan and bring to the
boil. Turn off the heat and leave to steep for at least 10 minutes while you
prepare all the other ingredients.

Add the shallots and thyme to a large saucepan with the butter and a
splash of olive oil, and gently sauté until the shallots are translucent,
about 5 minutes. Add the garlic and cook for a minute or two, then
add the chestnut and field mushrooms and cook slowly down until the
mushrooms are cooked through and juicy.

Remove the dried mushrooms from the stock, retaining both the
mushrooms and the stock. Finely chop the soaked mushrooms and
set aside.

Add the rice to the pan and stir in, making sure the rice is completely
coated in the mushroom, onion and butter mixture. Add the chopped
soaked mushrooms to the pan and stir in, then add half a ladleful of the
stock and stir in.

Continue to stir until all the stock has been absorbed, then add another
half ladleful of stock and keep stirring, adding the stock in small amounts
until the rice is cooked and all the stock absorbed. Don't be tempted to
rush the process – it takes time, about 45–50 minutes. The risotto should
be quite loose and the rice should still have a little bite when it's cooked.

Remove from the heat and stir in half the Parmesan, the cream cheese,
parsley and balsamic vinegar, if using. Add salt to taste.

Sprinkle over the remaining Parmesan and a little freshly ground black
pepper and serve immediately.

Vegetarian Moussaka

serves 6

Like a lot of people we try to eat meat-free a couple of times a week, and I find moussakas and lasagnes are often the easiest of recipes to make vegetarian whilst still being very delicious.

This recipe is one that Rebecca originally designed when she was at university and eating vegetarian food most of the time, with just a few adaptations.

20g dried porcini mushrooms
2 tablespoons olive oil
1 large onion, chopped
4 large garlic cloves, grated or
* finely chopped*
2 tablespoons dried oregano or
* mixed herbs*
1 cinnamon stick
1 medium aubergine, chopped into
* 1cm chunks*
250g chestnut mushrooms,
* roughly chopped*
1 large courgette, chopped into
* 1cm chunks*
1 x 390g pack passata
2 tablespoons tomato purée
500g white potatoes (King Edwards
* or similar)*
1 x 400g can of chickpeas, drained
sea salt and freshly ground
* black pepper*

For the sauce
500ml semi-skimmed milk,
* plus a little extra to mix with*
* the cornflour*
4–5 tablespoons cornflour
150g mature Cheddar, grated,
* plus extra for sprinkling on*
* top (optional)*
good grind of black pepper

Put the dried porcini mushrooms into a bowl and cover with 130ml boiling water.

Put the olive oil, onion, garlic, oregano, cinnamon stick, a good grind of pepper and a pinch of salt into a large pan over a low heat and cook until the onions are softened, about 5 minutes. Add the aubergines, chestnut mushrooms and courgettes to the pan, stir through and cook for a further 10 minutes, or until the courgettes start to soften.

Remove the dried mushrooms from the liquid, ensuring you retain the liquid, then roughly chop the mushrooms and stir into the vegetable mixture. Once browned, stir in the passata, tomato purée and the mushroom water and leave to simmer for 30 minutes, stirring occasionally.

Meanwhile, peel and slice the potatoes thinly by hand or using a mandoline, to about the thickness of a £2 coin. If the potato slices are thicker, you will have to cook the dish for slightly longer.

For the sauce, put the milk in a pan over a low heat and slowly bring to the boil. Mix the cornflour with 2 tablespoons of milk until the consistency of double cream, ensuring all the cornflour is mixed in. Add the cornflour mixture to the milk slowly, stirring continuously, until the sauce is the consistency of a thick custard. Remove from the heat and immediately stir in the grated Cheddar and black pepper.

Preheat the oven to 200°C/180°C Fan/Gas Mark 6.

Stir the drained chickpeas into the vegetables and continue to simmer for around 15 minutes, until the mixture is quite thick and most of the liquid has evaporated. Add salt and pepper to taste.

Spread half the vegetable mixture over the bottom of the dish. Dig out and discard the cinnamon stick (no one needs a mouthful of that!). Layer half the sliced potatoes across the top of the mixture as you would with lasagne sheets.

Carefully spoon over half the cheese mixture, spreading it until it covers the potato evenly.

Repeat the layering process, being careful to distribute all the ingredients evenly. The layers aren't overly thick but there should be enough to give an even bite of each layer in every mouthful. Sprinkle some more Cheddar on top, if desired.

Put into a preheated oven for 1 hour, until the potatoes are soft and the top browned.

Quail's Egg
Arancini

serves 6

I often make risotto at home, and any leftovers can be used in these extra-special arancini balls with a soft-boiled quail's egg in the middle. They make a great lunch or starter dish with a spinach or watercress salad. I usually make these with a vegetarian risotto, and the Mushroom Risotto on page 51 is a perfect match.

6 quail's eggs
approx. ½ bottle white wine vinegar
450g cold risotto (such as the Mushroom Risotto on page 51)
sunflower oil
*100g **gluten-free** plain flour*
2 large eggs
○ *100g polenta*

Prepare a bowl of ice-cold water and set aside. Boil the quail's eggs for exactly 2 minutes 15 seconds, then plunge them immediately into the iced water and leave for 5 minutes. Transfer the eggs to a clean bowl and cover with white wine vinegar. Leave for at least 15 minutes (the speckles will come off the shells), then peel. You can omit this step but the eggs will be much harder to peel.

Tear off a piece of clingfilm about A4 size. Place the clingfilm over your scales and weigh out 75g of risotto rice onto it.

Using the clingfilm as a base, flatten the rice to an even circle that will encase the egg. Pick the clingfilm up and use it to help the risotto encase the egg. Be careful as the eggs are fragile. Roll the risotto into a ball.

Heat a deep fat fryer or a deep pan of oil to 180°C.

Place the flour, eggs and polenta in three separate bowls. Roll the arancini in the flour, then the egg, and finally the polenta.

Deep fry for 4 minutes until golden, then transfer to kitchen towel for a couple of minutes to absorb any excess oil, and serve immediately.

Vegetarian Pie

I have been playing with the flavours of vegetarian food to make it more attractive for my family of meat eaters, and this is my favourite recipe so far. I love it, and it freezes well, which is a bonus. The ingredient list may seem long, but once it's prepped it's the simplest cooking process. I often make four individual pies, but you can make one large one (as per the image), if you prefer. This mixture is also lovely served with a cheesy mash if you don't want to make the pastry.

50g butter
1 tablespoon olive oil
1 medium onion, diced
2 garlic cloves, finely chopped
1 medium leek, diced
30g fresh basil, finely chopped
30g fresh flat-leaf parsley, finely chopped
10g fresh rosemary leaves, finely chopped
1 cinnamon stick
1 teaspoon caraway seeds
1 Granny Smith apple, cored and diced with skin on
2 heaped teaspoons rose harissa (or regular harissa)
120g sundried tomatoes, roughly chopped
1 x 400g can of chickpeas, drained
300ml **gluten-free** vegetable stock
2 bay leaves
1 small egg
1 tablespoon milk
1 x quantity Shortcrust Pastry (page 194)
50g mature Cheddar cheese, grated
sea salt and freshly ground black pepper

Preheat the oven to 200°C/180°C Fan/Gas Mark 6.

Heat the butter and oil in a frying pan over a low heat and gently fry off the onion, garlic, leek, herbs, cinnamon stick, caraway seeds and apple for 3–5 minutes, until the onion is translucent but not coloured.

Once cooked through, add the harissa, sundried tomatoes, drained chickpeas, stock and bay leaves. Add salt and pepper to taste, and continue to cook over a low heat until the mixture has reduced to a lovely rich sauce.

Transfer the mixture to four individual pie dishes (or one large dish), remove the bay leaves and allow to cool.

In a small bowl, whisk the egg and milk together. Roll out the pastry and cut out lids for the pies, then place on top and brush with the egg and milk mixture. Sprinkle over the grated Cheddar and cook for 20–25 minutes, until the pastry is crisp and golden and the filling is cooked through.

Harissa Mac
and **Cheese**

serves 6

If I fed Ben his favourite mac and cheese every day, he would be in heaven – I think it's the whole teenage carb-loading thing. This recipe is for my standard cheese sauce, which works perfectly every time with this quantity of pasta. The addition of harissa gives it a bit of spice and a lovely warming feel for those cold nights, however I have been known to throw leeks, ham, lots of vegetables and other things that need eating up into the pasta just before it goes into the oven – it's one of those wonderfully adaptable dishes.

400g **gluten-free** pasta; I use penne or fusilli as gluten-free macaroni can be hard to find
6 tablespoons cornflour
800ml milk, plus a little extra for making the cornflour paste
250g extra-mature Cheddar cheese, grated, plus extra for sprinkling
50g Parmesan, grated
○ 2 tablespoons harissa paste
pinch of sea salt

Preheat the oven to 200°C/180°C Fan/Gas Mark 6. Bring a large pan of water to the boil, add the pasta and parboil for 6–7 minutes; it needs to be about half-cooked. Drain the pasta and set aside.

Mix the cornflour with a little milk until it is the consistency of double cream.

Put the milk into a saucepan and bring to the boil, then reduce the heat to a simmer and slowly add the cornflour paste, stirring or whisking all the time. Keep stirring/whisking for a couple of minutes – the milk will thicken quickly but you need to cook out the cornflour.

Remove from the heat and immediately add the Cheddar and Parmesan. Beat in until you have a smooth, thick cheese sauce. Add the harissa paste and salt and stir in, then add the partially cooked pasta, stir through, and place in a baking dish.

Sprinkle over a little extra Cheddar cheese and place in the oven for 30 minutes, until golden and bubbling. This is best eaten as soon as you can without the cheese burning your mouth.

Beer-Battered Fish

serves 4

We all love fish and chips, but the only time Ben can eat them is when we stay with his sister in Macclesfield, where they have a gluten-free option at the fish and chip shop. So I have learnt to make my own delicious version at home. This batter is very thick, so coating the fish is the trickiest part – I submerge mine on both sides, then hold it up to allow a little to drip off, then drop it carefully into the oil.

250g **gluten-free** plain flour, plus extra for dusting
50g cornflour
2 teaspoons **gluten-free** baking powder
sunflower oil, for frying
330ml bottle of ice-cold **gluten-free** lager; I used Peroni
4 x 150g skinless, boneless white fish fillets
sea salt and freshly ground black pepper

Place a little flour for dusting the fish in a bowl and season with salt and pepper. Lightly dust the fish fillets with the seasoned flour.

Sift the 250g flour, cornflour, baking powder and salt into a large bowl.

Fill a deep frying pan one-third full with oil and heat to a temperature of 180°C. If you don't have a thermometer, simply drop a little cube of bread into the pan; if it sinks then rises, sizzling, your oil is hot enough. The oil needs to be deep enough for the fish to be able to cook without touching the bottom of the pan, but watch out that it's not so deep that it splashes over the top of the pan. Alternatively, use a deep fat fryer.

Quickly mix the ice-cold beer into the sieved flour and dunk both sides of the fish fillets in the batter. When evenly coated, plunge the fish carefully into the oil. I cook only one or two at a time, depending on the size of the pan; don't be tempted to overload the pan as the temperature will plunge.

The fish should only take a few minutes to cook. The batter will be light golden in colour, however fish varies dramatically in size and thickness, so please watch cooking times carefully. If in doubt, pierce with a cocktail stick to test if the fish is cooked through – if there is any resistance, give it another minute or so.

Remove the fish onto kitchen towel to drain, and serve immediately (with chips!).

Pan-Fried Cod, Simple Mustard Sauce, Wilted Spinach and Mashed Potato

serves 4

This is a lovely dish, which I serve as a quick supper. Harry is forever dipping his finger in the sauce, so I have to hide it! The sauce also well with pork, too.

I know a lot of people don't like to cook fish, but this just takes minutes. I keep a stash of toothpicks next to the cooker, which I use to test food, particularly fish.

500g potatoes (King Edwards are good for mashing)
50g butter
400ml double cream
○ *3–4 tablespoons wholegrain mustard*
1–2 teaspoons lemon juice
olive oil
4 x 150g skinless cod fillets (haddock or any white fish will work just as well)
500g baby spinach
sea salt and freshly ground black pepper

Peel and boil the potatoes for about 12 minutes until soft, then mash with a little of the butter and set aside.

My Tip
The perfect ratio for a buttery mash is 70 per cent potato to 30 per cent butter, which is wonderful for special occasions; I tend not to add as much butter in my day-to-day cooking!

Pour the double cream into a saucepan and bring to the boil, then reduce the heat and simmer for about 5 minutes until the cream has thickened. Add 3 tablespoons of the wholegrain mustard, 1 teaspoon of lemon juice and a pinch of salt. Taste, adding more mustard, lemon juice and salt until you are happy; I like mine quite acidic, but it's up to you. Once you are happy with the seasoning, set aside ready to reheat just before serving.

Add a good splash of oil to a pan to heat. Season the cod fillets, then place one into a hot pan – don't move it around – add a knob of butter and leave the fish alone. You will see it change colour from translucent to white at the side of the portion; once the colour change is about halfway up the side, flip the fish over. Don't fiddle with the fish in the pan as it will break up; watch the side of the fish again and when you can see no more translucent bits, use a cocktail stick to check there is no resistance in the thickest part of the fish. Remove from the pan to a warm plate and continue until all the fish is cooked. Don't overcook it – so much depends on the thickness of your fish, but if you watch it closely and don't move it around you should have perfect fried fish every time.

Put the spinach in a pan and pour over boiling water to cover. Leave to stand for 2 minutes, then drain. Chop the spinach finely, pressing out as much water as you can.

To serve, gently reheat the sauce. Put some mash in the middle of the plate with spinach over the top and the cod to one side. Pour over the sauce.

Chilli Prawn Pasta

This dish is the perfect quick and easy supper dish, which we all need after a busy day sometimes. I prefer the sweeter taste of cold water prawns, but if you prefer the larger jumbo Asian prawns, you can use these.

*400g **gluten-free** spaghetti*
1 bird's eye chilli, finely chopped
2 garlic cloves, crushed
1 tablespoon olive oil
1 x 400g can of cherry tomatoes
500g Atlantic cold water prawns
10g fresh flat-leaf parsley,
  finely chopped
sea salt and freshly ground
  black pepper

Bring a large pan of salted water to the boil. Add the spaghetti to the rapidly boiling water and cook to your personal preference; I like mine a little al dente.

Gently fry off the chilli and garlic in the olive oil for a couple of minutes, taking care not to colour the garlic. Add the can of tomatoes to the chilli mixture and simmer gently for 5–8 minutes, until thickened. Season with salt and pepper to taste.

Add the prawns to the chilli and tomato mixture and gently simmer until cooked through. Add most of the chopped parsley and stir through, reserving a little to serve.

Drain the pasta and add to the sauce, tossing it with the sauce and prawns. Sprinkle over the extra parsley and serve.

Oven-Roasted
Sea Bass

serves 3–4

Quick to prepare and easy to make, this dish is packed full of flavour. Serve on its own or with a large green salad.

1 onion, chopped

50ml olive oil, plus a little extra for frying

350g cherry tomatoes; I used the plum variety

50g olives; I used pitted black olives from a jar, but go with your favourite, green or black

2 garlic cloves, chopped

20g flat-leaf parsley, roughly chopped, plus extra to serve

4–5 sprigs of fresh thyme, roughly chopped, plus extra to serve

grated zest and juice of 1 lemon

450g cooked new potatoes, cut into bite-sized chunks

2 whole seabass, gutted and descaled, approx. 350g each

sea salt and freshly ground black pepper

Preheat the oven to 180°C/160°C Fan/Gas Mark 4.

Gently sauté the onions in a frying pan in a little oil for a few minutes, then transfer to a deep roasting tin with two-thirds of the olive oil, the cherry tomatoes, olives, garlic and two-thirds of the herbs. Pour over most of the lemon juice and all the zest, and season with salt and pepper. Add the cooked potatoes and toss together so everything is coated.

Place in the oven, uncovered, for 15 minutes.

Stuff the fish with the remaining herbs, then place on top of the vegetables in the tin and drizzle over the remaining oil and lemon juice and a little more salt and pepper.

Cover with tin foil and return to the oven for 18–20 minutes, until the fish is easily pierced with a toothpick in the thickest part. Serve immediately, straight from the pot, or plate up with the fish on top of the vegetables and sprinkled with a few fresh herbs.

My Tip
Make sure you pour the cooking juices over the top of the sea bass – they're delicious and really add to the dish.

hassle free, gluten free

Cheesy Pasta Bake with Smoked Haddock and Prawns

I'm a huge fan of one-pot dishes that I can just stick in the oven. This one is also a great way to get children to eat fish, by hiding it in their pasta! And it's an economical way of serving fish, as a little goes a long way.

300g **gluten-free** fusilli pasta
200g broccoli, cut into
    bite-sized pieces
600ml milk, plus a little extra for
    making the cornflour paste
6 tablespoons cornflour
400g mature Cheddar cheese, grated
150g frozen peas
150g small Atlantic prawns
    (these can be frozen)
400g skinless, boneless smoked
    haddock fillet, cut into
    bite-sized pieces
sea salt and freshly ground
    black pepper

Bring a large pan of salted water to the boil and cook the pasta and broccoli together for 5 minutes. Drain and set aside.

Preheat the oven to 200°C/180°C Fan/Gas Mark 6.

Bring the milk to the boil in a pan and add a good grind of black pepper.

Put the cornflour into a mug with enough milk to make a paste – it should be the consistency of double cream. Slowly add the cornflour mix to the boiling milk, whisking all the time. Keep boiling for 60 seconds, making sure the milk does not catch on the base of the pan.

Remove the thickened milk from the heat and immediately add the cheese and whisk until a thick sauce is achieved.

Place the pasta, broccoli, peas, prawns and smoked haddock pieces in a deep baking dish and mix carefully so the ingredients are evenly distributed. Pour the cheese sauce mixture over the top, but do not stir through.

Cook for 25 minutes, until the cheese is bubbling and golden. Remove from the oven and serve immediately.

Confit Turkey
Leg Rissoles

makes about 12

So many people buy turkey crowns now, but I noticed that turkey legs are really cheap, so I worked on creating this recipe, which gives such a flavour punch and can be used as an alternative to stuffing, or served as little nibbles or starters with cranberry sauce.

For the confit

2 x 250g packs unsalted butter
1 x 800g turkey drumstick
4 bay leaves
5–6 sprigs of fresh thyme
½ bulb of garlic (cut the bulb horizontally through the centre to show the cross section)
½ teaspoon green peppercorns (or black if not available)
sunflower oil

For the rissoles

100g finely chopped shallots
2 tablespoons oil (from the confit mixture)
200–225g turkey drumstick meat (from the confit mixture)
3–4 sprigs of fresh thyme, leaves picked
½ bulb garlic (from the confit mixture)
2 large eggs
100g **gluten-free** plain flour
100g fine polenta
sea salt and freshly ground black pepper

Preheat the oven to 170°C/150°C Fan/Gas Mark 3.

Melt the butter in an ovenproof casserole dish and place the turkey drumstick into the dish with the other confit ingredients. If the butter doesn't cover the turkey leg, just add a little sunflower oil. Place in the oven for 4 hours, then remove from the oven and leave to cool.

For the rissoles, sauté the shallots in the oil from the confit mixture for about 5 minutes, until soft and translucent. Remove from the heat and allow to cool.

Remove the bone and sinew from the drumstick and gently shred the meat into fine strands; it should be melting and just fall apart. Add to a bowl with the thyme leaves. Take 4–5 of the soft cloves of garlic from the halved garlic bulb and add to the meat with the cooked shallots. Add salt and a really good grind of black pepper. Taste and adjust the seasoning if desired. Add 1 egg and mix in.

Flatten the mixture into the bottom of the bowl and divide roughly into twelve portions. Roll each portion into a small ball about the size of a table tennis ball. If serving as nibbles you may want to make them a little smaller for bite-sized pieces. Place on a baking tray, then transfer to the fridge for 30–40 minutes until cold.

Place the flour into a shallow bowl, then place the polenta into a second bowl, and beat the remaining egg in a third bowl. Gently roll the balls in the flour, then the egg, then the polenta, and place on a tray.

Fill a heavy-based pan one-third full with oil and heat to a temperature of 180°C. If you don't have a thermometer, simply drop a little of the mixture into the pan; if it sinks then rises, sizzling, your oil is hot enough. Alternatively, use a deep fat fryer. Cook the rissoles in small batches – I do them in batches of four until golden and crispy, about 3–5 minutes.

Creamy Chicken and **Summer** Vegetable Pie

serves 6–8

This is an incredibly delicious and indulgent pie that I often cook when we have friends over for supper. The list of ingredients looks long, but once it's prepped it's very simple and means I am not rushing around last minute when the guests arrive. I suggest serving with mash and cabbage.

1 large onion, chopped
1 loose-packed teaspoon fresh thyme
  leaves (or dried mixed herbs)
2 tablespoons vegetable oil
1 litre **gluten-free** chicken stock
150g chopped chestnut mushrooms
750g chicken breast, chopped into
  bite-sized pieces
1 red pepper, chopped
150g frozen sweetcorn
150g frozen peas
200ml double cream
6 level tablespoons cornflour
100ml milk
2 x quantities Shortcrust Pastry
  (page 194)
1 egg, beaten
sea salt and freshly ground
  black pepper

You will need
a 30cm oblong baking dish

Preheat the oven to 200°C/180°C Fan/Gas Mark 6.

Put the onion, herbs and oil into a large stock pot or saucepan and gently sauté until the onion is translucent and tender.

Add the stock, mushrooms and chicken to the pot and simmer very gently for 15–20 minutes, until the chicken is cooked through but tender. Don't be tempted to turn up the heat; you don't want the chicken to be tough. Add the red pepper, sweetcorn, peas and cream and remove from the heat.

Strain the creamy sauce from the chicken and vegetables into a separate pan, and transfer the chicken and veg into the baking dish. Mix the cornflour with the milk to make a smooth paste like double cream.

Put the creamy chicken stock back onto the hob and heat through until nearly boiling. Give the cornflour mix a quick stir to recombine, then add to the creamy stock. Stir, then leave to simmer for 3–5 minutes, until the sauce is thick. Season with salt and pepper.

Pour the thickened sauce over the chicken and veg and stir through until everything is evenly coated and you have a nice moist pie filling. Set aside the remaining sauce to use as gravy for the completed dish.

Roll out about two-thirds of the pastry and carefully place over the pie, leaving a good 1cm overhanging the edge. I use a china blackbird or upside down ceramic egg cup to hold up the pastry in the centre of the pie. Once covered, cut off the excess pastry and use it to patch any tears. Brush the pastry with the beaten egg and place into the oven for 40–45 minutes, until the pastry crust is golden and crispy.

Remove from the oven and leave to cool for a few minutes.

Chicken Pie with **Chestnuts** and **Bacon**

serves 8–10

I love making this large, deep pie during autumn, but what I really enjoy is being able to serve a gluten-free pie without my guests knowing! I serve this with creamy mash and broccoli for an ideal dinner.

2 medium onions, chopped
1 leek, chopped
250g smoked lardons
6 skinless, boneless chicken thighs, chopped into bite-sized chunks
1 teaspoon dried sage
500ml **gluten-free** chicken stock
150g vacuum-packed chestnuts, chopped
2 tablespoons cornflour
250ml double cream
2 x quantities Shortcrust Pastry (page 194)
1 egg, separated
sea salt and freshly ground black pepper

You will need
a 24cm springform tin

Gently fry the onion, leek and lardons in a frying pan for about 5 minutes until the onion and leek are softened. Add the chicken and sage to the pan and fry for a further 5 minutes until browned. Add the chicken stock and chopped chestnuts and bring to the boil, then simmer for a further 7–8 minutes, until the chicken is cooked through but still soft and juicy.

Mix the cornflour with a little cold water to a smooth paste (the consistency of double cream) and stir into the chicken mixture until thickened. Do this slowly so there are no lumps. Add the cream and season with salt and pepper to taste, then set aside to cool.

Preheat the oven to 190°C/170°C Fan/Gas Mark 5. Roll out two-thirds of the pastry to a circle the thickness of a 10-pence piece, ensuring it's big enough to cover the base and sides of the tin (see Tip, page 194).

Line the base and sides of the tin with the rolled-out pastry. Gluten-free pastry is softer than regular pastry, so can be a little fiddly to work with; please keep some offcuts in case you need to patch bits. Line the pastry case with baking parchment and fill with baking beans, then blind bake for about 15–20 minutes, until the base is crispy. Remove from the oven and allow to cool, then remove the baking beans and paper.

Take a small piece of the remaining pastry and roll it into a thin sausage shape, then lay this around the top edge of the blind-baked pastry base, using a little egg white to stick it down.

Fill the case with the chicken and chestnut filling, using a slotted spoon and a little of the sauce to keep it moist. Reserve the rest of the sauce to use as gravy when you serve the dish.

Roll out the remaining pastry to form a lid and place over the pie, fluting the edges. Egg wash using the egg yolk. Place in the oven for 20 minutes, until golden brown on top, but note that it will never be as golden as non-gluten-free pastry so don't overcook it. Remove from the oven, allow to cool slightly, then remove from the tin and serve with the reserved gravy.

Chicken Stir-Fry

serves 4

One of the best things I have is a very large non-stick wok, which I use for stir-fries at least once a week – I can make a filling, healthy meal for all six of us in under thirty minutes! However, a lot of standard Chinese ingredients contain wheat, which can make getting that intensity of flavour a little hard. I know the addition of my store-cupboard favourite pomegranate molasses looks odd here, but it adds a real rich sweetness to the dish. Oomi noodles are a new discovery, and I really love them – they are gluten free, high in protein, instant no-cook noodles; but you can serve this with Egg Fried Rice (page 206) or plain rice.

The trick with stir-fries is to chop everything before you start cooking. This marinating technique stops the meat becoming very dry when cooking, and while it's marinating I can chop up all the other ingredients.

3 chicken breasts
1 large egg, separated
2 tablespoons cornflour
splash of sunflower oil
1 onion, chopped
1 chilli, chopped; I used a bird's eye chilli (remove the seeds or use a less spicy chilli, if preferred)
4 garlic cloves, finely sliced
75ml **gluten-free** soy sauce
2 tablespoons pomegranate molasses
300ml **gluten-free** chicken stock
200g tenderstem or purple sprouting broccoli, chopped
1 large red pepper, deseeded and chopped
200g chestnut mushrooms, chopped
460g **gluten-free** noodles (optional); I use Oomi noodles

Thinly slice the chicken breasts using the grain of the chicken to guide you. In a small bowl, combine the egg white and cornflour, then add the chicken and completely coat it in the mix. Leave to marinate for 15 minutes.

Put a small splash of oil in your wok or frying pan, add the onion and chilli and fry, stirring occasionally, until the onion is translucent and cooked through, about 5 minutes.

Add the garlic, soy sauce, pomegranate molasses and chicken and continue to stir until the chicken is just cooked but still soft and tender, about 3–5 minutes in a wok.

Add the chicken stock and broccoli and cook quickly over a high heat for 2–3 minutes; you may need to add a little water.

Add the red pepper, mushrooms and egg yolk and fry for a further 2–3 minutes, then add the noodles, if using, and cook through until the noodles are warm. Serve immediately.

My Tip
I try to avoid using balsamic vinegar in recipes, as it varies a great deal in terms of flavour: a really expensive one is wonderful served with bread and olive oil, but the cheaper ones can be very acidic and harsh. I don't want to put very expensive balsamic vinegar in recipes, which is why I use pomegranate molasses in a lot of dishes: it's cheap, readily available and of a standard quality.

Mutton Curry

serves 4

I have an ideal quick midweek Vegetable Curry recipe (page 50), but it's really nice to spend time slow cooking a curry for something a little more special. I use mutton here, which I love for the richness and depth of flavour it gives; it really is a wonderful meat for slow cooking. I am lucky enough to be able to source mutton easily, but you can buy it online, or if you prefer you can use diced lamb shoulder instead; I would suggest reducing the cooking time by 30 minutes if using lamb.

2 tablespoons sunflower oil
800g diced mutton
*500ml **gluten-free** lamb or chicken stock (ready-made, not a stock cube)*
75ml coconut milk from a can, plus a little extra to serve (optional)
1 tablespoon lemon juice
2 teaspoons sea salt
Turmeric, Sultana and Coconut Basmati Rice (page 207), to serve

For the spice mix
3 x star anise
1 teaspoon fennel seeds
2 teaspoons coriander seeds
1 teaspoon cumin seeds
8 cardamom pods

For the curry paste
25g fresh turmeric (or 1 teaspoon turmeric powder)
25g fresh ginger (or ½ teaspoon ground ginger)
450g chopped onions
1 x 390g pack passata
8–10 garlic cloves
2 whole red chillies

You will need
a 3-litre ovenproof lidded casserole dish

Preheat the oven to 180°C/160°C Fan/Gas Mark 4.

Dry fry all the ingredients for the spice mix in the casserole dish until fragrant, then grind to a powder using a pestle and mortar and set aside. Heat the oil in the same casserole dish (don't wash it up as it all adds to the flavour) over a medium heat and brown off the mutton. Remove from the pan and set aside.

Using a stick blender or food processor, blend the curry paste ingredients to a paste, then add to the ground spice mix and fry in the (unwashed) casserole dish for 15–20 minutes. You start with a vibrant red colour and end up with a deep umber-coloured paste, about a quarter or less of the original mixture. I use a flat-sided wooden spoon to scrape off any bits that are sticking to the bottom of the casserole dish; as this reduces down, you can't really leave it as you don't want the curry paste to burn.

Once the paste is reduced, add the mutton to the mix with the lamb stock. Stir in well, add the coconut milk, lemon juice and salt and place the lid on the casserole dish, then transfer to the preheated oven for 2 hours, or until the meat is soft and tender.

Check the seasoning – you may need to add a little more lemon juice or salt. You can also streak some more coconut milk through for effect, if you want to, just before bringing to the table.

My Tip
I remove this curry from the oven, leaving the lid on the casserole dish after I have adjusted the seasoning, then I start to cook the rice. This gives the meat time to rest and ensures that it's lovely and hot but not mouth-burning.

Lamb and Feta Sliders with Olive Mayonnaise

serves 6

Everyone loves a good burger, and a good home-made one served with salad is one of life's joys. I make slider buns using my Focaccia recipe (page 181) and a muffin tin. Ordinary beef burgers are lovely, but these are my favourite alternative.

1 x quantity focaccia dough
   (page 181)
1½ tablespoons olive oil, plus extra
   for greasing
1 onion, finely chopped
3 garlic cloves, minced
1½ teaspoons chopped fresh oregano
   (or 1 teaspoon dried)
600g lamb mince
1 large egg
120g feta, cut lengthways then
   widthways into 6 equal pieces
sea salt and freshly ground black
   pepper

For the olive mayonnaise
25g olives (I use pitted black olives
   from a jar)
○ 75g mayonnaise
lemon juice
chopped flat-leaf parsley and basil

Make up the focaccia dough and lightly oil six holes of a standard muffin tin. Divide the dough among the oiled holes (it's easier to spoon it in as it's very soft). Gently smooth the surface of the buns with a damp hand. Loosely cover with oiled clingfilm and allow to prove for 1 hour.

While the focaccia is proving, gently sauté the onion, garlic, oregano, salt and pepper in the olive oil for 5 minutes until the onion is soft.

Leave to cool, then combine with the lamb mince and egg. Split the mixture into six equal portions.

Take one of the squares of feta and encase it in one of the portions of mince, making a nice burger. Repeat with the remaining feta and mince mixture.

Once the focaccia has proved, lightly brush with olive oil and sprinkle with a little salt then place in the oven for 20–25 minutes, until golden.

Meanwhile, use a stick blender or food processor to combine the olives with the mayonnaise, a little lemon juice to taste and some chopped herbs.

When the bread has been cooked and cooled, cook the burgers on a barbecue or in a frying pan for 7–9 minutes; they should be juicy and a little pink on the inside. I like to serve the burgers with the olive mayonnaise, lettuce, and the Pepper Salad on page 201. Tomatoes are wonderful too.

My Tip
When cooking burgers, please resist the temptation to press down on the top of the burger. You are just pressing out moisture, when what you want to do is sear the burger over a high heat in the same way you would a piece of steak, and then gently cook it through, leaving it to rest for at least 5 minutes before eating.

Lamb, Rose Harissa and Apricot Kebabs

serves 4

On a nice sunny weekend, you can stick these on the barbecue and serve them with a selection of salads – my preference is for a jewelled chickpea salad. These can easily be prepared a day in advance to save time.

○ *2 heaped tablespoons rose harissa*
2 tablespoons lemon juice, plus a
little extra for drizzling
1 teaspoon sea salt
350g lamb neck fillet, cut into
16 bite-sized pieces
16 dried apricots
sprig of fresh thyme
1 red onion
olive oil

You will need
4 wooden skewers, soaked in water

Combine the rose harissa, lemon juice and salt in a bowl. Add the lamb and stir through to coat in the marinade, then leave to marinate for 2 hours.

Cover the dried apricots with boiling water and add the thyme. Leave to sit for 20–30 minutes until the apricots are plump and juicy.

Chop the red onion into quarters, then split the segments.

Assemble the kebabs: start with a cube of lamb, then an apricot, then some red onion, and continue until you end with the fourth onion segment.

Cook on a barbecue until the lamb is pink, about 12 minutes. Remove from the heat and leave to rest for 5–10 minutes. Just before serving, pour a little olive oil, lemon juice and the juices from the rested lamb over the final dish.

hassle free, gluten free

Lamb Meatballs in **Olive** and **Tomato Sauce**

serves 4–6

Meatballs are a great way of getting kids involved in cooking food, although we have ended up with some rather odd shapes over the years! These are a little more complex, but I think well worth the effort, and we often serve them in a big bowl with spaghetti when friends come over for supper. I make them up in big batches and freeze them for an easy standby meal. I buy large jars of black pitted olives in brine and use them in breads, savoury biscuits and casseroles; I find them a really useful store cupboard ingredient.

For the meatballs

3–4 *large garlic cloves, minced*
1 *onion, finely chopped*
1 *tablespoon olive oil*
1.6kg *lamb mince*
2 *tablespoons dried mixed herbs*
1 *large egg*
1 *teaspoon sea salt*
400g *mozzarella cheese (or feta or goat's cheese, if you prefer), chopped into small chunks*
sunflower oil, for frying
black pepper

For the sauce

1 *carrot*
1 *medium onion*
4 *garlic cloves*
1 *tablespoon olive oil*
1 *tablespoon dried mixed herbs*
500ml *chicken stock*
250ml *passata*
1 *x 450g jar of pitted black olives in brine: you will need 250ml brine and 50g olives, chopped*

To serve

gluten-free *spaghetti*

To prepare the meatballs, gently sauté the garlic and onion in the olive oil until translucent, about 5 minutes, then leave to cool.

Place the mince, herbs, egg, salt and a good grind of pepper in a large bowl, add the cooled onion and garlic mixture and combine well using your hands. Take approximately 40g of the meat mixture and wrap it around a chunk of cheese. Repeat with the remaining meat and cheese; I usually end up with between 25 and 30 meatballs (depending on who is helping!). Place on a tray in the fridge until required.

For the sauce, grate the carrot, onion and garlic straight into the saucepan, add the olive oil and herbs and sauté gently for 5 minutes. You can finely chop the onion if you prefer.

Add the chicken stock, passata, olives and brine and cook for about 15 minutes until reduced by about a third. You can use the sauce like this, or I like to blend it using my stick blender – not to a completely smooth sauce, but to something a little less chunky.

Heat a couple of centimetres of sunflower oil in a deep frying pan. Gently brown off the outside of the meatballs (they are going to cook in the oven, so don't worry too much if they're not cooked through – you just want to seal them at this stage). I do this in batches and place on kitchen towel, then transfer them all to a casserole dish.

Preheat the oven to 190°C/170°C Fan/Gas Mark 5. Pour the sauce over the meatballs and sprinkle over any remaining cheese. Place in the oven for 20 minutes. Remove from the oven and allow to rest. I like to serve this with spaghetti and salad.

Crispy Lamb Ribs
with **Spicy Basil Marinade**

serves 4–6

This is one of my favourite marinades – I use it on all cuts of lamb, and on chicken and pork too, but I particularly love it on lamb ribs. You can chop the marinade ingredients by hand, but it's much easier to use a stick blender or food processor.

Lamb ribs can be tricky to find, but you can ask your local butcher to cut them for you, and I can also get them in my local supermarket. These are wonderful cooked on the barbecue, but you can also cook them in the oven; the cooking time is dependent on the size of the chops, as they can differ greatly, so I have just given a rough estimate. The ribs should be lovely and crispy when served.

100g fresh basil
6 garlic cloves
3–4 tablespoons lemon juice
4 red chillies; I use standard chillies rather than bird's eye, but please adjust to your preferred level of spiciness
1 tablespoon salt, plus extra to sprinkle
75–100ml olive oil
650–750g lamb ribs (try to buy the larger, meatier ones if available – this should give you around 12–16 ribs)
sea salt

Preheat the oven to 180°C/160°C Fan/Gas Mark 4.

Using a food processor or stick blender, blend 75g of the basil, stalks included, with the garlic, 2–3 tablespoons of lemon juice, 3 whole chillies, 1 tablespoon of salt and 75ml olive oil.

Cover the lamb ribs liberally with the marinade and rub in. Cover and leave to marinate for at least 2 hours.

Cook on a barbecue for 25 minutes, or in a large roasting tray in the oven for approximately 45 minutes, depending on the size and thickness of the ribs.

Once cooked, place on a large serving platter and drizzle over some olive oil and lemon juice, then leave to rest for 10–15 minutes.

Deseed and finely chop the remaining chilli, and place in a bowl. Finely shred or tear the remaining basil leaves and combine with the chopped chilli. Pour off the meat juices and combine with the basil and chilli, then drizzle over the ribs, sprinkle over some salt if desired and serve immediately.

Top left: spinach, garlic and chilli roast tomato salad (page 200); right: braised garam masala shoulder of lamb (page 84) and turmeric, garlic and salt-crusted roast potatoes (page 210)

Braised Garam Masala Shoulder of Lamb

serves 4–6

This is a shorter version of the lamb I cooked in the MasterChef final. I am really proud of this, and it makes a lovely alternative roast dinner. I like to serve it with the Turmeric, Garlic and Salt-Crusted Roast Potatoes (page 210) and the Spinach, Garlic and Chilli Roast Tomato Salad (page 200).

1.5kg shoulder of lamb (I like to buy the easy-carve joint, if possible)
6 anchovy fillets, roughly halved
4 garlic cloves, thinly sliced
250g natural yogurt
1½ teaspoons ground cumin
○ *1 teaspoon garam masala*
1 teaspoon turmeric powder
1 teaspoon hot chilli powder
1 tablespoon lemon juice, plus extra for drizzling
1 teaspoon sea salt
olive oil, for drizzling

To serve
Turmeric, Garlic and Salt-Crusted Roast Potatoes (page 210)
Spinach, Garlic and Chilli Rosat Tomato Salad (page 200)

Using a sharp knife, pierce the lamb all over and push the anchovy fillets and garlic slices into the holes.

Combine all the remaining ingredients to create a marinade (add any leftover garlic slices) and smear it over all sides of the lamb. Place on a baking tray, cover with foil and leave to marinate for 1–2 hours.

Preheat the oven to 180°C/160°C Fan/Gas Mark 4. Cook the lamb for 90 minutes, then remove the foil and cook for a further hour.

Remove from the oven and leave the meat to rest on a chopping board. Meanwhile, combine the pan juices with a little extra olive oil and lemon juice, to taste, and keep warm (the yogurt may have split a little but it should combine well to form a gravy). Serve the lamb with the meat juices drizzled over, and the roast potatoes and spinach and tomato salad on the side.

Moussaka

serves 6

This is one of my absolute favourites – I love it served with Focaccia (page 181) and a big green salad. Moussaka doesn't traditionally have potato in it, but I like to add it to a one-pot dish, especially when feeding hungry teenagers.

2 tablespoons olive oil
1 large onion, chopped
4 large garlic cloves, grated or finely chopped
2 tablespoons dried oregano or mixed herbs
1 cinnamon stick
1 medium aubergine, chopped into 1cm chunks (if you don't like aubergine you can substitute mushrooms instead)
500g lamb mince
1 x 390g pack passata
2 tablespoons tomato purée
500g white potato (King Edwards or similar)
sea salt and freshly ground black pepper

For the sauce
500ml semi-skimmed milk, plus a little extra to mix with cornflour
4–5 tablespoons cornflour
150g mature Cheddar, grated, plus extra for sprinkling

Put the olive oil, onion, garlic, oregano, cinnamon stick, a pinch of salt and a good grind of black pepper into a large pan over a low heat and cook until the onions are softened, about 5 minutes.

Add the aubergine and stir in, then add the mince, making sure it is broken up, and continue to cook, stirring occasionally, until it's evenly browned.

Stir in the passata, tomato purée and 130ml water and leave to simmer for 30 minutes, stirring occasionally. Season to taste.

For the sauce, put the milk in a pan over a low heat and slowly bring to the boil.

Mix the cornflour with about 2 tablespoons of milk until almost the consistency of double cream, ensuring all the cornflour is mixed in. Add the cornflour mixture to the milk slowly, stirring continuously, until the sauce is the consistency of a thick custard. Remove from the heat and stir in the grated Cheddar and a good grind of black pepper.

Thinly slice the potatoes to about the thickness of a £2 coin; you can do this by hand or with a mandoline. If you make the slices thicker, you will just have to cook it for slightly longer.

Spoon half the mince mixture into the bottom of the dish (discard the cinnamon stick) and layer half the sliced potatoes across the top. Carefully spoon over half the cheese mixture, spreading it evenly until it covers all the potato. Repeat the layers, being careful to distribute everything evenly. The layers aren't overly thick, but there should be enough to give an even bite of each layer in every mouthful.

Sprinkle some Cheddar on top and place in the oven for 1 hour, until the potato is soft and the top brown.

Chilli Pork
Spare Ribs

serves 4

We eat these all year round, often as starters or nibbles, but sometimes with the Egg Fried Rice on page 206 for a light supper. They pack a real flavour punch and are so easy to make – everything is prepared straight into one pan on the hob.

1 x 750g rack of baby back pork ribs, chopped into individual ribs
3 tablespoons sunflower oil
1–2 red chillies, finely chopped
1cm piece of fresh ginger, grated
4 garlic cloves, finely chopped
○ *3 tablespoons golden syrup or runny honey (I prefer syrup as it gives the stickiness without the distinctive honey flavour)*
2 tablespoons dry sherry or rice wine
140g tomato purée
*4 tablespoons **gluten-free** dark soy sauce (I use Clearspring tamari soya sauce)*
finely sliced red chilli and spring onion, to serve (optional)
sea salt

Place the ribs into a large wok or non-stick pan with a lid. Measure out the 3 tablespoons of oil (don't wash the measuring spoon) and add to the pan with a good pinch of salt.

Add the chillies, ginger and garlic, and use the oily measuring spoon to measure out the golden syrup or honey (this stops it sticking to the spoon and makes life much easier).

Finally, add the sherry, tomato purée, dark soy sauce and 125ml water, and use a spatula to mix all the ingredients together until the ribs are well coated in sauce.

Put the lid on the pan, place it over a low heat and cook for around 1 hour, stirring every 20 minutes to ensure the ribs are evenly coated; check more regularly towards the end of the cooking time to ensure they're not burning. The ribs need to be a dark red caramel colour with a thick sauce; when tested with a knife the meat should be really tender so it comes away easily from the bone.

Leave the ribs to sit, covered, for 10–20 minutes, then serve directly from the wok or pan, or transfer to a serving platter, sprinkled with finely sliced chilli and spring onion.

My Tip
To test the heat of a chilli, I cut the green top off and put it to the tip of my tongue; I can usually ascertain the heat from this touch. Another method of controlling the heat of chillies is to leave the chilli whole, just slice down the middle, and place it in the dish while cooking; as soon as the dish is the right heat for me, I remove the whole chilli.

Smoked Paprika-Marinated Belly of **Pork** with Crispy Crackling

serves 4

I get the belly of pork from my butcher, and he takes the ribs out individually for me, which I use to add flavour to the Butterbean, Thyme and Garlic stew on page 202. He then scores the top so I can get lovely crackling. If buying from a supermarket, try to get a thicker piece of pork from the meat counter; they will score it for you there.

2 tablespoons smoked paprika
3 tablespoons lemon juice
1.2–1.5kg belly of pork, plus a
   couple of ribs for cooking
sunflower oil
sea salt

To serve
Butterbean, Thyme and Garlic Stew
   (page 202)
cavolo nero

Preheat the oven to 230°C (210°C Fan/Gas Mark 8).

Combine the paprika, lemon juice and 1 teaspoon of salt in a bowl and rub it into the underneath of the belly of pork an hour or two before cooking. Leave the pork to marinate, rind side up, uncovered in the fridge or in a cool place so the rind can dry out.

Just before placing the pork in the oven, rub the rind lightly with oil and sprinkle liberally with sea salt. Place on a lightly oiled baking tray and roast for 20 minutes, then reduce the heat to 180°C/160°C Fan/Gas Mark 4 and continue to cook for 90 minutes. I leave it alone and try not to open the oven door – and don't baste so you get that lovely crispy crackling.

 I serve this in wide bowls with the butter beans at the bottom, a square or strip of the pork belly on top, and some simply cooked cavolo nero on top.

hassle free, gluten free

Pork and
Fennel Pasta

A local Italian restaurant introduced a gluten-free menu about five years ago, and they quickly became a favourite destination for us as a family. Ben always ordered the spicy fennel sausage pasta, and this is my version of that dish – probably not authentic, but he loves it and I hope you do too. This sauce makes double the quantity required, so I split it in two and freeze half the mixture for future use.

400g **gluten-free** fusilli pasta
freshly grated Parmesan, to serve

For the sauce
2 teaspoons fennel seeds
1 tablespoon olive oil
1 large red onion, chopped
1 red chilli, finely chopped; I used a
  bird's eye chilli, which is very spicy
2 bay leaves
1 tablespoon dried mixed herbs
3–4 garlic cloves, chopped
900g pork mince
2 x 390g packs passata
250ml **gluten-free** chicken stock
1 teaspoon sea salt

Dry fry the fennel seeds for a couple of minutes in a saucepan, then use a pestle and mortar to grind them to a powder.

Add the olive oil, onion, ground fennel seeds, chilli and herbs to the same saucepan and cook over a medium heat for about 5 minutes until the onion is translucent. Add the garlic and cook for another couple of minutes.

Add the pork mince and mix through, then cook for about 5 minutes until the mince is well browned.

Add the passata, chicken stock and salt to the pan and simmer for 45 minutes.

Once cooked, leave the sauce to stand for 15–20 minutes or the pork mince can be tough (if the sauce has been frozen and slowly reheated, the mince should not be tough). I use this time to cook the pasta.

Bring a large pan of water to the boil and cook the pasta according to the packet instructions.

Drain the pasta and stir through the sauce, then sprinkle with some freshly grated Parmesan. I like to serve this in a large bowl at the table so everyone can help themselves, with some more grated Parmesan and a big green salad.

Pork Chop, Apple and **Red Onion** with Sage Yorkshire Pudding

serves 4

This is an economical dish, using the boneless pork loin chops you can find in most supermarkets and butchers. It's based on a dinner my nan used to cook; she used lamb chops in the Yorkshire pudding batter, but this makes for a more expensive midweek supper, so I have gone for pork.

1 red onion, roughly chopped
1 Braeburn or Granny Smith apple,
  cored but not peeled,
  roughly chopped
vegetable oil
2–3g very finely chopped fresh sage
  (or 1 teaspoon dried sage if fresh is
  not available)
2 × quantities Yorkshire pudding
  batter (page 192)
4 boneless pork loin chops
good grind of black pepper

To serve (optional)
gravy
green vegetables

Preheat the oven to 220°C/200°C Fan/Gas Mark 7.

Place the red onion and apple chunks in the bottom of a non-stick metal roasting tin, add enough oil to cover the base of the tin, and cook for 10 minutes.

Add the fresh sage to the Yorkshire pudding batter and stir to combine. Remove the tin from the oven and, working quickly, add the pork chops, covering each one with equal amounts of the apple and onion and a good grinding of black pepper. Pour over the batter and return to the oven for 25 minutes (please don't peek).

Open the oven door to release the steam, then reduce the heat to 190°C/170°C Fan/Gas Mark 5 and cook for a further 5 minutes to set the Yorkshire pudding.

Remove from the oven and serve with vegetables and a gluten-free gravy.

Fillet Steak with Horseradish and Crème Fraîche Cannellini Beans

This is a lovely all-year-round meal for those special occasions, but I particularly like it during the summer when I can barbecue the steak. The marinade works equally well on any cut of steak that you would use for frying or a barbecue.

750g fillet steak
sunflower oil
sea salt and freshly ground
   black pepper

For the marinade
100ml crème fraîche
○ 2 tablespoons horseradish sauce
3–4 sprigs of thyme, leaves picked
1 garlic clove
1 tablespoon lemon juice

For the horseradish and crème fraîche cannellini beans
2 x 400g cans of cannellini beans,
   drained and rinsed
200ml crème fraîche
15g flat-leaf parsley leaves
½ garlic clove, minced
2 tablespoons olive oil
1 tablespoon lemon juice
○ 2 tablespoons horseradish sauce
   (see page 212 for homemade)
½ teaspoon sea salt

For the garlic and herb sauce
520g flat-leaf parsley, leaves picked
½ garlic clove, minced
4 tablespoons olive oil
lemon juice, to taste (start with
   1 tablespoon and add more to
   your taste)

Combine all of the ingredients for the marinade with a little salt and pepper. Place the beef fillet in a shallow bowl, cover with the marinade and leave to marinate for 1–2 hours.

For the beans, combine all the ingredients in a large bowl, then adjust the seasoning to taste – you may wish to add more lemon juice and salt.

For the sauce, combine the parsley, garlic and olive oil, then add lemon juice and salt and pepper to taste.

Preheat the oven to 220°C/200°C Fan/Gas Mark 7.

Heat a splash of oil in a frying pan over a high heat. Once hot, sear all the sides of the steak and then place in the oven for about 16–18 minutes for medium rare; if you have a very long, thin piece of meat, the cooking time will be shorter.

Once cooked, rest the steak for at least 15 minutes before carving into thick slices.

Arrange the beans on a plate, place the carved steak on top and drizzle over the garlic and herb sauce.

My Tip
If you are unsure of how to cook meat perfectly, always sear it first as this seals in the juices and adds a layer of flavour. Oil and season the joint, then place it in a hot pan and turn until all the sides are a nice dark golden colour. Then continue to cook as normal.

dinner, supper and food for guests

Beef Stew

serves 6–8

This is a version of the traditional beef stew that my nan used to cook every Friday night when my younger brother and I used to go to her house for tea, while mum and dad were on the market stall. It's a slow-cook recipe, so great to prepare in the morning and just leave to cook over the course of the day; you could even make it a day or two in advance, store it in the fridge and slowly reheat when required.

Use shin of beef if you can – stewing steak is good, but I find this cut of meat superior. Most supermarket meat counters and high street butchers will stock it, and it's not an expensive cut. The list of ingredients looks long, but please don't be put off – once it's in the pot it cooks itself.

1kg shin of beef, diced into
  bite-sized pieces
1 teaspoon sea salt
1 teaspoon black pepper
splash of sunflower oil
2–3 stalks celery, diced
  (about 100g)
2 carrots, diced
1 leek, diced
1 large onion, diced
3–4 large garlic cloves,
  finely chopped
5g fresh thyme leaves
3 bay leaves
50ml cooking brandy (or red wine)
*750ml–1 litre **gluten-free***
  beef stock
250ml tomato passata
1 tablespoon pomegranate molasses
4 tablespoons cornflour

Preheat the oven to 150°C/130°C Fan/Gas Mark 2). Season the meat with the salt and pepper.

In a large ovenproof stock pot with a lid, fry off the meat in batches in a splash of oil until golden brown and the edges are caramelised, about 10–12 minutes. Remove each batch with a slotted spoon into a large bowl and repeat until all the meat has been browned. This should be done in batches, taking your time, as the caramelisation really adds to the flavour.

Add the vegetables and herbs to the pot and stir through the meat juices. Put the lid on, stir occasionally, and gently cook down for about 15 minutes, until the vegetables are soft. Remove the vegetables with a slotted spoon and place on top of the meat.

Turn up the heat under the pot, add the brandy and, using a wooden spoon, scrape all of the lovely caramelised bits off the bottom of the pan into the brandy. Keep cooking the brandy until it is syrupy – about a tablespoon of liquid – and there is no harsh alcohol smell.

Return the vegetables and meat to the stock pot, add the beef stock until it covers the meat – in my pot this is around 750ml, but you might need a little extra – then add the passata and pomegranate molasses and stir in. Finally, combine the cornflour with a little water to create a paste (it should be the consistency of double cream) and stir in well.

Put the lid on the stock pot and place in the oven for 4 hours. I try to remove the lid about 40 minutes before the end of cooking, as I find the sauce can be a little thin.

My Tip
This can also be made on the stove top. You will just need to keep an eye on it and stir regularly, so it's not quite as straightforward as sticking it in the oven for a few hours.

Once the stew is removed from the oven, replace the lid and leave to rest for at least 30–40 minutes – the perfect time to cook your accompaniments. I like to serve this with mash and cabbage or other dark green veg. While serving, remove the bay leaves if you can find them, otherwise warn the guests!

My Tip
Throughout the book I have tried to reuse store-cupboard ingredients such as the pomegranate molasses – there is nothing worse than buying an ingredient and it languishing in the cupboard for years. If you don't have the pomegranate molasses, balsamic vinegar will also work.

souping it up

I wanted to show you how I cook, and often this involves using the same recipe in different ways – for example, the Butternut Squash and Rosemary Dip (page 121) can also be used as a lovely purée alongside both chicken and pork; it's works brilliantly in both guises.

This chapter follows that concept with classic flavour combinations, usually things I keep in my cupboard and freezer as staples, just souped up and used in different ways. Once you know a flavour combination works, you can use it to experiment with different techniques and ideas.

COD and CHORIZO

Smoked Cod and Chorizo Nibbles

makes about 24

These are a little fiddly, but they are really lovely served on their own as nibbles, or with a romesco sauce or Sriracha mayonnaise as a starter.

Alternatively, you can make them into fishcakes and serve them as part of a lunch or dinner. It is one of those versatile recipes I love to have to hand. I nearly always have smoked haddock in the freezer, as well as a chorizo ring in the fridge, so I can put these together quite quickly if needed.

50g chorizo, sliced into rings the thickness of a £1 coin
175g smoked haddock or cod fillets
milk, to cover the fish
2 large eggs
300g cold mashed potato
50g manchego cheese, finely grated
½–1 tablespoon lemon juice
*100g **gluten-free** plain flour*
○ *100g fine polenta*
sunflower oil, for frying
sea salt

Place the chorizo in a frying pan and fry for 3–5 minutes, until crispy, but be careful as it does burn quickly. Do not add oil as the chorizo lets out a beautiful orange oil of its own. Remove from the heat and set aside.

Put the fish fillets in a pan and cover with milk. Gently poach the fish over a low heat until the fish flakes easily and is no longer translucent, about 6–7 minutes. Remove the fish from the milk and, when cooled, gently flake, removing the skin if necessary and checking for bones.

Chop the fried chorizo or put it in a blender and blitz to a crumb. Retain the chorizo cooking oil.

In a large bowl, combine 1 egg, the mashed potato, chorizo crumb, chorizo oil from the pan, manchego cheese and fish. I try to keep some lumps of fish so it has texture. Add the lemon juice and salt to taste.

Carefully roll the mixture into small ping-pong-sized balls and place on a plate. Refrigerate for about 1 hour until the balls are set.

Place the flour in a shallow bowl, the polenta in a second bowl and beat the remaining egg in a third bowl. Gently reshape the balls if necessary, and coat first in the flour, then in the egg, then in the polenta, and return to the fridge.

Fill a heavy-based pan one-third full with oil and heat to a temperature of 180°C. If you don't have a thermometer, simply drop a small cube of bread into the pan; if it sinks then rises, sizzling, your oil is hot enough.

When ready to serve, fry off the balls in batches until crispy, about 3–4 minutes. Note that these won't go a dark golden brown, so don't overcook.

Left: spiced almonds (page 19)
Right: smoked cod and chorizo
nibbles (page 101)

Butterbean Soup
with **Smoked Cod**
and **Chorizo**

serves 4

Cod and chorizo is a favourite flavour combination of mine; I always keep frozen fish handy in my freezer, as it's quick to defrost for an easy supper. Chorizo rings are great as well, as they provide a real flavour punch, and you can keep them for a long time; they are perfect to fry up with tomato for a quick pasta dish, or to use in the following recipe.

200g smoked cod; I use undyed, but it's up to you
600ml milk
50g unsalted butter
2 bay leaves
2 banana shallots, finely diced
5g fresh thyme leaves
2 × 400g cans butter beans, drained and rinsed
100g chorizo, roughly chopped
splash of olive oil
splash of lemon juice
pinch of sea salt (be careful, though, as the fish and chorizo are naturally salty)
freshly ground black pepper

Put the fish into a pan with the milk, butter and bay leaves and gently poach until the fish is cooked through but still holding its shape, about 6–8 minutes depending on the thickness of the fish; it is cooked when it flakes gently and can be easily pierced with a toothpick.

Meanwhile, sauté the shallots in a pan with the thyme until translucent, about 5 minutes. Try not to colour them as you want a nice white soup. Once the fish is cooked, drain the milk into a saucepan with the shallots and thyme, and set the fish aside.

Add the butterbeans to the pan and simmer for 8–10 minutes, until the liquid is reduced by about a third.

While the butterbeans are simmering, gently fry off the chorizo in a splash of olive oil. You want it crispy on the outside, but it does burn quickly so watch it carefully – it will only take a few minutes. Once crispy, allow it to cool, then remove from the pan, reserving the orange oil. Chop the cooked chorizo into a crumb; it is sprinkled over the soup so should not be too chunky.

Place the butterbean mixture into a food processor, or use a stick blender, and blend until smooth. Add a little lemon juice and season to taste.

To serve, pour the butterbean soup into four bowls. Add a quarter of the smoked cod to the centre of each bowl, sprinkle over the chopped chorizo and drizzle over some of the chorizo oil.

My Tip
I always keep cans of pulses in my cupboard, to pad out stews, soups and curries when you need to make things go a bit further. They are really good for you and make the most wonderful instant soups.

Smoked Cod and Chorizo Fishcakes with **Manchego Cheese**

serves 4

These make a great alternative to regular fishcakes. The manchego gives a subtle cheesy flavour to the dish which I really enjoy, but feel free to use another hard cheese if you prefer.

400g smoked cod
milk, to cover the fish
knob of butter
1 bay leaf
400g cold mashed potato; I used
    leftovers, so mine already has
    butter and seasoning in it
75g chopped chorizo, gently fried
    until crispy
grated zest and juice of 1 lemon
○ 75g mayonnaise
50g manchego cheese, finely grated
    (if you can't find this, use
    Parmesan instead)
75g **gluten-free** plain flour
2 eggs
200g **gluten-free** breadcrumbs
    (page 195) or polenta
sunflower oil, for frying
sea salt and freshly ground
    black pepper

Place the fish in a pan and cover with milk. Add the butter and bay leaf and poach the fish gently for 6–7 minutes, until it is flaky (test it with a cocktail stick). Remove the fish from the milk and discard the milk.

In a large bowl, combine the mashed potato, fried chorizo, lemon zest and juice, mayonnaise and manchego cheese with a little salt and pepper.

Gently flake the fish into the potato mixture and fold it in, trying not to break up the chunks of fish but ensuring an even distribution of the fish through the mixture. Flatten the fishcake mixture to the bottom of the bowl and divide it up like pizza to ensure even portions.

My Tip
This mixture will make four large fishcakes but you could make smaller ones, if you prefer, and they freeze well.

Place the flour, eggs and breadcrumbs into three separate bowls.

Take one portion of fishcake mixture and gently roll it into a ball – it is quite loose so be gentle. Roll the ball in the flour, then in the egg, then in the breadcrumbs. Put the fishcake on to a plate and gently flatten it into a fishcake shape. Repeat with the remaining portions of fishcake, then cover the plate with clingfilm and leave to set in the fridge for an hour.

Once the fishcakes have set, heat a shallow layer of oil in a frying pan (the oil should come about halfway up the fishcakes) until a little of the mixture sizzles when dropped in. Gently fry off the fishcakes in the oil, turning after about 5 minutes, until golden brown and cooked all the way through.

Roast Cod with a Chorizo and Herb Crumb with Roast Cherry Tomatoes

serves 4

This is the final recipe featuring cod and chorizo. I often serve this to family and friends, and even those who are not overly keen on fish enjoy this pairing. It's really not complicated, and the end result is lovely.

olive oil
4 x 150–200g cod loin fillets
12 cherry tomatoes
40g chorizo, chopped

For the crumb
75g chorizo, chopped
120g **gluten-free** breadcrumbs
   (page 195)
10g fresh coriander, roughly chopped,
   plus extra to serve
5g fresh basil, roughly chopped
grated zest of ½ lemon
1 tablespoon olive oil
sea salt and freshly ground black
   pepper, to taste

Preheat the oven to 200°C/180°C Fan/Gas Mark 6.

Place all the crumb ingredients into a food processor and use the pulse setting to mix it all together. You don't want a powdery crumb but something with a little texture. Alternatively you could finely chop the chorizo and mix it with the rest of the crumb ingredients.

Put a little olive oil into the bottom of a roasting dish and place the cod on top, turning it in the oil so both sides are coated. Divide the crumb topping into four and press a portion onto each fish fillet, covering the top with a thick crumb. You might have a little left over – it depends on the size of the fillets.

Put the tomatoes in the roasting dish with the fish, and sprinkle around the chopped chorizo. Place in the oven for 10–12 minutes, until the fish is cooked through. Pierce the fish with a cocktail stick – if there is any resistance it needs another couple of minutes.

Serve the fish with the roast tomatoes and chorizo from the pan, along with some of the orange cooking oil, then sprinkle over some chopped coriander. I serve this with creamy mash and green vegetables or a lovely big salad.

BEETROOT and POMEGRANATE

Beetroot and Pomegranate Reduction

makes about
75–100ml

Beetroot works so well with forest fruit flavours such as blackberry, but my favourite pairing – beetroot and pomegranate – is a bit off the wall! I have used it here to show how, with a few simple twists, you can create some lovely flavour combinations that are different, easy and can be real show-stoppers.

A few years ago, every dish was covered in a balsamic glaze. This is a similar concept, wonderful drizzled over trout or salmon, ham, and my particular favourite game meats, duck, goose and venison. You can prepare it in advance and it will keep in the fridge for a week. I put mine in a squeezy bottle for easy use, but a spoon and jar work just as well.

500ml beetroot juice (available from supermarkets)
4 tablespoons pomegranate molasses

Place the juice and molasses in a saucepan over a low heat, and bring to a gentle simmer; don't be tempted to turn the heat up, as you want to retain that beautiful deep purple colour, rather than turning it brown.

Simmer for 30–40 minutes, until you have a syrup which coats the back of a spoon. You can also test the consistency by splashing some on a plate – if it retains its shape and doesn't flood the plate, it's done.

Cool and place in a suitable bottle for use. You may find that you need to place the bottle in warm water to loosen the sauce before use.

Roasted Beetroot with **Pomegranate Molasses**

serves 6

When I was younger, the only food I would not eat (apart from stuffed hearts – still gross, sorry mum) was beetroot. I have horrible memories of salads just awash with the stuff that comes pickled in jars, and white bread sandwiches stained bright pink. However, in the last few years I have had a revelation: roasted beetroot, raw beetroot and home-pickled beetroot are delicious.

This is my favourite way of cooking it. It involves store-cupboard essentials and can be served in lots of different ways – I use my stick blender to blend it to a purée, and my food processor to make it into instant chutney, lovely with cold turkey and ham; I can even warm it through quickly to use as a vegetable. It's perfect to make and keep in the fridge over busy times like Christmas.

500g peeled red beetroot, cut into similar-sized wedges
3 tablespoons pomegranate molasses
50g unsalted butter
5g fresh thyme sprigs
good pinch of sea salt

My Tip

I use disposable gloves when peeling beetroot, as the colour can stain.

Preheat the oven to 190°C/170°C Fan/Gas Mark 5. Tear off two large sheets of tin foil and lay them out in a cross shape large enough to wrap all the beetroot wedges in.

Place the wedges on to the foil and drizzle over the pomegranate molasses, then add the butter, thyme and salt. Wrap them all in the foil, making sure there are no holes for leaks, and place in the oven for approx. 1½ hours, until tender and you can pierce the beetroot wedges with a cocktail stick.

Use immediately, or leave to cool then store in a sealed container in the fridge for 3–4 days.

hassle free, gluten free

Beetroot and Pomegranate with **Feta Mousse**

serves 6–8

I originally devised this dish for a pop-up I was doing with Atul Kochhar, as the *amuse-bouche* on the menu. This is a simpler version, but the flavours are beautiful together and the colour is something really special.

*1 x quantity Feta Cheese Mousse
   (page 14)*
*1 x quantity Roasted Beetroot
   (page 112)*
*1 x quantity Beetroot and
   Pomegranate Reduction (page 111)*
fresh pomegranate seeds, to garnish
a few fresh thyme leaves, to garnish

To serve (optional)
Focaccia (page 181)

Place a large swirl of the feta cheese mousse on a plate with the warm roasted beetroot. Drizzle the reduction around the plate and sprinkle with pomegranate seeds and a few fresh thyme leaves.

Serve with focaccia, if using.

Venison with Pomegranate Roasted Beetroot and Fondant New Potatoes

serves 4

This is a truly special dish to serve for dinner, which does not take too long to cook. Everything except the venison and the sauce can be prepped in advance and gently warmed through in the microwave just before serving. I like to serve this with blanched curly kale dressed with butter and black pepper.

800g loin of venison
splash of sunflower oil
knob of butter
sprig of fresh thyme
½ bulb of garlic, split into cloves
sea salt and freshly ground
    black pepper

For the sauce
125ml red wine
500ml **gluten-free** beef stock
knob of butter
pomegranate molasses (optional)

For the fondant potatoes
450g new potatoes
75g unsalted butter
4–5 sprigs of fresh thyme, plus extra
    for sprinkling
2 garlic cloves, crushed
splash of sunflower oil
250ml **gluten-free** chicken or
    beef stock

To serve
1 x quantity Roasted Beetroot with
    Pomegranate Molasses (page 112)
1 x quantity Beetroot and
    Pomegranate Reduction (page 111)
cooked buttered kale

Preheat the oven to 180°C/160°C Fan/Gas Mark 4. If necessary, remove the venison from the fridge and allow it to come to room temperature. Gently oil the meat, sprinkle with salt and pepper and set aside.

For the fondant potatoes, top and tail the new potatoes and cut in half. Don't worry about peeling them, but make sure they are scrubbed clean and all roughly the same size.

Place the potatoes in a frying pan (if this can go in the oven, it makes life a little easier) with the butter, thyme, garlic cloves and a splash of oil. Season with salt and pepper and gently sauté for 7–8 minutes, until the bottom of the potatoes are a lovely deep golden colour.

My Tip
I always add a splash of oil to the pan when cooking in butter as it stops the butter from burning.

Turn the potatoes over and add the stock to about three-quarters of the way up the potatoes; the exact quantity will depend on the size of your pan.

Place the pan in the oven and cook until the stock has nearly evaporated and the potatoes are soft and tender, about 45 minutes. Remove from the oven, season lightly and sprinkle with a little chopped thyme. If necessary, set aside to be warmed through when plating.

Increase the oven temperature to 220°C/200°C Fan/Gas Mark 7.

About 25 minutes before serving, heat a non-stick frying pan until really hot, but don't oil the pan. Place the lightly oiled venison in the pan and sear (page 93), then add a knob of butter, the thyme and garlic and baste with the cooking juices. Place in the oven for 7–9 minutes for medium rare; this will depend on the thickness of your meat. Remove the meat and set aside to rest for 15 minutes, reserving the meat juices to add to the sauce.

My Tip
Cooking times will depend upon the thickness of the meat, but venison has no fat so cooks really quickly and is best served on the redder side of medium rare. Remember it will continue to cook when resting. Use a meat thermometer if you're unsure, or test a piece; it should feel as though you are pressing the fleshy part at the base of your thumb.

Add the red wine to the pan and bring to the boil to reduce. When there is about a tablespoon of wine left, add the stock and meat juices from the rested meat and continue to simmer (don't boil) until a thick sauce is achieved. Add a knob of butter and season. If you feel the sauce is lacking a little flavour you can add a drop of pomegranate molasses.

Serve straight away with the sliced venison, fondant potatoes, roasted beetroot, beetroot reduction and some buttered kale.

BUTTERNUT and ROSEMARY

Butternut Squash and **Rosemary Dip** with **Sriracha Oil** and **Bacon Crumble**

makes about 600g

A very different dip, served with a spicy chilli oil and bacon crumble. I serve it with the Flat Breads on page 190 and crudités. The dip is lovely warm, but can also be eaten cold. This makes a good-sized bowl of dip, so is great for a buffet-style meal. Alternatively, you can use it as a purée, served with chicken or pork.

250g chopped butternut squash
5–7g fresh rosemary, on the stalk,
   plus 3–4 fresh rosemary leaves,
   finely chopped
*250ml **gluten-free** chicken or*
   vegetable stock
pinch of sea salt
1 x 400g can of butterbeans,
   drained and rinsed
1 tablespoon olive oil
○ *splash of Sriracha chilli sauce*
4 rashers streaky bacon, grilled until
   crispy and chopped finely

Place the squash, rosemary stalks, stock and salt into a small saucepan, so the stock covers the squash, and simmer gently until the stock is nearly gone and the squash tender, about 15 minutes, but do make sure the squash is meltingly tender. Drain the excess water.

Remove the rosemary stalks (the leaves can stay in) and add the drained butterbeans. Blend until smooth using a stick blender or food processor, then transfer to a serving bowl.

Combine the olive oil and Sriracha and drizzle over the top of the soup, then sprinkle with the bacon and rosemary leaves.

See page 125 for photograph.

Butternut Squash Soup with Bacon and Rosemary

serves 4

In the summer when the children came home from school, I would make up a tray of carrots, cucumber, red pepper, grapes, hummus, and any other vegetable they would eat raw, as it stopped them snacking on rubbish. In the winter I made big bowls of soup – it's a fantastic way to use up any extra vegetables you have in the bottom of the fridge, and is quick and easy to cook. This is a real favourite – I think it's the bacon, to be honest...

200g rindless smoked streaky bacon
475g butternut squash, peeled and cut into chunks
1 onion, chopped
7g fresh rosemary, on the stalk
olive oil
*750ml **gluten-free** chicken or vegetable stock*
250g potato, cubed (King Edwards are ideal)
cream cheese (optional), to garnish
sea salt and freshly ground black pepper

Take 75g of the bacon and fry in a pan for about 5 minutes, until crispy and golden. Chop finely and reserve.

In a large saucepan, place the butternut squash, the remaining bacon, the onion, rosemary and a splash of olive oil. Gently fry until the butternut squash is starting to brown.

Add the stock, potato and a little salt and pepper, and simmer until the potato is completely cooked through, about 7 minutes. Remove the rosemary stalks (don't worry if some leaves have fallen off, we just don't want the thick woody stalks) and discard.

If you have a liquidiser, carefully transfer the soup into that and blitz until smooth. Alternatively, you could just mash the soup by hand or place in a food processor. Add salt and pepper to taste.

Place in bowls with a spoonful of cream cheese, if using, and sprinkle over the crispy bacon bits.

Rosemary and Garlic Roasted Chicken with **Butternut** and Rosemary Purée

serves 4

To me, chicken is the ultimate easy food. I often put a chicken in the oven midweek, with some jacket potatoes or a few vegetables, and I have a great meal with minimum input. However, this recipe is just a little bit special, so maybe for a Sunday lunch or dinner with friends.

1 x 1.5kg chicken
½ garlic bulb (sliced horizontally to create a cross section)
½ lemon
10g rosemary, on the stalk
drizzle of olive oil
50g butter
sea salt and freshly ground black pepper

To serve
1 x quantity Butternut Squash and Rosemary Dip with Sriracha Oil and Bacon Crumble (page 121); prepare all 3 elements, but leave them separate
Chicken Gravy (page 209)
green vegetables
Turmeric, Garlic and Salt-Crusted Roast Potatoes (optional, page 210)

Preheat the oven to 180°C/160°C Fan/Gas Mark 4. Place the chicken in a roasting tray and put the halved garlic bulb into its cavity. Squeeze the lemon over the chicken and then place the squeezed out half inside the cavity.

My Tip
I always untruss a chicken to cook it, as I find that this way you get lovely, melt-off-the-bone legs and tender breast meat.

Remove about twenty leaves from the rosemary and chop finely, then set aside. Place three-quarters of the remainder of the rosemary in the cavity of the chicken; if some is sticking out, that's fine. Place the last quarter under and around the bird.

Drizzle some olive oil over the chicken and sprinkle liberally with salt, black pepper and the finely chopped rosemary. Dot the butter liberally over the chicken and place in the oven for approximately 90 minutes, until the chicken juices run clear when the thigh is pierced.

To serve, carve the chicken, then put a good smear of the butternut squash dip onto each plate, drizzle with the Sriracha oil (optional) and sprinkle over the chopped bacon. Place the chicken to the side and serve with some gravy, a green vegetable of your choice and some roast potatoes.

Butternut Squash and **Rosemary** Fondants

serves 4

These make a wonderful alternative to potatoes. I like to serve fondants as I can prep them in advance and warm them up in a microwave just before serving, or leave them in the oven with no last-minute running around. They are lovely as a side dish or as a vegetarian starter with a beetroot leaf salad and a sprinkle of blue cheese. If you're serving them as a side, they are particularly good served with pork, but work well with almost any roasted meat.

50g butter
splash of vegetable oil
4 peeled rounds from the neck of a butternut squash (approx. 70g), about 1.5cm thick
10g fresh rosemary, on the stalk
200ml **gluten-free** fresh chicken or vegetable stock (not a stock cube as it's too salty)
sea salt and freshly ground black pepper

Preheat the oven to 180°C/160°C Fan/Gas Mark 4.

Put the butter and a splash of oil in an ovenproof frying pan with the butternut squash rounds. Bruise the rosemary by twisting it, then add to the pan. Sprinkle over a little salt and pepper and cook gently until the base of the fondant is a lovely golden brown, about 6–8 minutes. Don't be tempted to turn the heat up: the sugar in the squash makes it easy to burn, and you want to infuse the rosemary flavour into the squash.

My Tips
When frying in butter, which adds flavour as well as colour, always add a splash of oil as this stops the butter burning.

If you don't have an ovenproof frying pan, you can transfer the squash to a roasting tin, but you will lose some of the flavour.

Flip the fondants over and add the stock to the pan to about two-thirds of the way up the squash. Place in the oven for 25–30 minutes, until tender and easily pierced with a toothpick. Serve the fondants caramelised side up, sprinkled with a little sea salt and black pepper.

desserts

Peanut Butter Cheesecake

serves 8–10

I make no apologies for this cake – it is laden with calories in every way! It is, however, Ben's favourite, and I make it for very special occasions. It is not difficult, as the only cooking involved is melting the chocolate for the topping. Feel free to decorate the top of the cheesecake with crushed peanut brittle, chocolates, gold leaf – whatever takes your fancy! – or just leave it plain. If desired, you can halve the mixture and make individual cheesecakes in muffin trays – they're great fun, although a little fiddly.

*300g **gluten-free** digestive-type biscuits; I use 2 packs of gluten-free Hob Nobs*
150g unsalted butter, melted
*1 x 340g jar of **gluten-free** crunchy peanut butter (I like the texture, but use smooth if you prefer)*
280g cream cheese
2 teaspoons vanilla bean paste
125g icing sugar
150ml double cream

For the topping
*100g **gluten-free** dark chocolate, 70 per cent cocoa solids, finely chopped*
100ml double cream

You will need
a 25cm non-stick springform cake tin

In a food processor, blitz the biscuits to a fine crumb. Combine the blitzed biscuit crumbs with the melted butter, then use the mixture to line the bottom and halfway up the sides of the tin. Place in the fridge for 30–40 minutes until set and hard.

Put the peanut butter, cream cheese, vanilla bean paste and icing sugar into a food processor and whizz until fully combined; alternatively you can use an electric hand whisk for this.

In a separate large bowl, whisk the double cream until soft peaks appear. Take a tablespoon of the peanut butter mixture and, using a spatula, gently fold into the cream, trying to retain as much air in the mix as possible. Repeat until all of the peanut butter mixture is incorporated into the cream.

Add the mix on top of the crumbed biscuit base, being careful not to disturb the sides. Place in the fridge and chill for 2–3 hours until set. You can freeze this now, or keep it covered in the fridge for up to 48 hours.

For the topping, place the chocolate in a large bowl. Heat the cream in a pan until just boiling, then pour over the chocolate and whisk until the chocolate is melted and the mixture is smooth.

Take the cheesecake straight from the fridge and pour over the ganache, working from the centre outwards. Return to the fridge for 30 minutes or until the chocolate is set.

Remove the cheesecake from the tin – you will probably need to carefully run a knife around the edge of the cake – and serve.

Raspberry, Peach and **Almond** Cobbler

serves 6–8

This recipe is inspired by the peach cobblers you find in America, where there is often a glut of peaches. In the UK peaches and nectarines are expensive, so I use frozen peach slices, but drained canned peaches will work just as well. It's a great alternative to pastry and is perfect served with gluten-free vanilla ice cream or whipped cream.

*500g frozen peach slices
  (or drained canned)*
400g frozen raspberries
1½ tablespoons golden caster sugar
50g flaked almonds

For the cobbler
125g softened unsalted butter
225g golden caster sugar
1 large egg
1 teaspoon vanilla extract
*250g **gluten-free** plain flour*

My Tip
My freezer is always full of frozen fruit, whether it is from mum and dad's garden or from the supermarket. It's cheaper to use than fresh, readily to hand, and just as good in desserts if cooked as fresh. In fact, I think frozen fruit is better for smoothies as there is no need to add ice, which waters down the fruit.

Preheat the oven to 200°C/180°C Fan/Gas Mark 6. Place the frozen fruit in the bottom of a pie dish and combine well. Sprinkle over the caster sugar and set aside.

Make the cobbler by beating the butter and sugar together with an electric whisk until creamy. Add the egg and vanilla extract and whisk in. Finally, whisk in the flour and you should end up with a stiff, wet batter.

Using a dessertspoon, place the mixture evenly over the fruit, then carefully spread it out using a fork or the back of the spoon. You might not get to the edges but try to ensure equal thickness where possible. Sprinkle over the flaked almonds.

Transfer to the oven and bake for 50–60 minutes, until the crust is golden brown. Remove from the oven and leave to rest for 10 minutes before serving.

My Tip
Always double check that the cobbler is cooked in the thicker parts, as otherwise you will end up with runny bits. Poke a toothpick into the cobbler and if it comes out clean then it's fine, but if it is sticky return it to the oven for another few minutes.

Chinese-Style
Caramel Pineapple

makes about 24

We all love the caramel fruits at the end of a Chinese meal, but they were a big no-no for Ben, so I decided to try and cook my own. A bit naughty and a little fiddly, but a real crowd pleaser!

100g **gluten-free** plain flour
1 teaspoon **gluten-free** baking powder
75ml milk
2 egg whites
450g fresh pineapple, core removed and cut into bite-sized chunks (about 24)
sunflower oil, for frying
○ ice cream, to serve (optional)

For the caramel
350g white granulated sugar
50g butter
60g toasted sesame seeds

Combine the flour, baking powder and milk in a bowl. Lightly whisk the egg whites until just at soft peak stage, then mix into the flour mixture to form a batter. In batches of about five, coat the pineapple pieces evenly in the batter.

Fill a heavy-based pan one-third full with oil and heat to a temperature of 180°C. If you don't have a thermometer, simply drop a little of the batter into the pan; if it sinks then rises, sizzling, your oil is hot enough. Alternatively, use a deep fat fryer.

Fry for 5–6 minutes, turning halfway through to get an even golden colour. Transfer the fried pineapple pieces onto a tray or bowl lined with kitchen towel and set aside.

Make the caramel by placing the sugar and 3 tablespoons of water into a heavy-based saucepan over a low heat. You can gently agitate the pan, but do not stir. Watch the pan carefully – the sugar will start to turn a golden brown; keep agitating the pan until all the granules have dissolved. You cannot hurry this process.

Once all the sugar has dissolved, carefully add the butter and stir in, then add the toasted sesame seeds and stir through. Turn off the heat. Put the battered pineapple pieces into the sesame caramel mix and very carefully toss until completely coated.

Remove the pieces one by one and plunge into a bowl of iced water, then transfer to a non-stick baking sheet. You will need to leave them for about 10 minutes for the caramel to completely harden, then serve on their own or with ice cream and eat immediately.

My Tip
Caramel should always be made with granulated sugar, caster just doesn't work for me. The pan you use will have a big impact on your caramel – don't be tempted to use non-stick pans, and persevere! Once you've mastered caramel you won't look back.

Cherry, Chocolate Frangipane Tart

serves 8

Cherries and chocolate are an absolutely classic match, and this tart is wonderful served hot or cold. Feel free to add a shot of alcohol to the cherry compote if serving for adults.

1 x quantity Sweet Shortcrust
   Pastry (page 194)
100g dark sweet cherries, to garnish
25g flaked almonds, to garnish

For the cherry compote
350g dark sweet cherries
50ml water (or alcohol for adults
   – almond or cherry flavour both
   work well)
1 tablespoon golden caster sugar
splash of lemon juice
○ 1 heaped tablespoon ready-made
   chocolate fudge icing (optional)

For the frangipane
150g butter, softened
150g caster sugar
1 large egg
150g ground almonds
○ 2 tablespoons dark cocoa powder

You will need
a 23cm loose-bottomed tart tin

Make the cherry compote by placing all the ingredients except the chocolate icing into a saucepan and simmering over a low heat for 5 minutes until a thick compote is achieved. There should be very little moisture left, but it should not be completely dry. Remember you are placing frangipane mix on top, so if it is too wet it will squelch up the sides and spoil the tart. If using the chocolate icing, stir in until dissolved, then leave to cool.

Roll out the pastry and use it to line the tart tin. Line the pastry case with baking parchment and fill with baking beans, then blind bake for 20 minutes. Set aside to cool.

Make the frangipane by whisking the butter and sugar together in a bowl until light and fluffy. Add the egg and whisk in, then gently fold in the ground almonds and cocoa powder. Alternatively, place all the frangipane ingredients into a food processor and combine until light and fluffy.

Preheat the oven to 190°C/170°C Fan/Gas Mark 5. To make the tart, place the cooled compote in the base of the blind-baked tart case and smooth out evenly. Add the frangipane on top; I do this in dollops then smooth with a spatula or palette knife. Gently press the cherries into the top of the frangipane to garnish, and sprinkle with the flaked almonds.

Place in the oven for 50–60 minutes, until risen and cooked through when tested with a cocktail stick. Serve warm or cold.

My Tip
I always kept a tub of ready-made chocolate fudge icing in the cupboard for those days when I suddenly discovered there was a bake sale at school or I needed to knock up a quick cake for something last minute. I know it's cheating, but sometimes it was just necessary – I always wished I was one of those super-organised people! A tablespoon added to the cherry compote here adds a wonderful chocolate hit, but the tart will still be delicious without it.

Crumble Topping

makes 350g
(enough to cover a
24cm rectangular
pie dish)

I find crumble topping so convenient and easy to make, a real stress-free alternative to pastry if you are in a hurry. This can of course be used as a traditional topping for cooked fruit, or sprinkled over gluten-free ice cream, and it also adds fabulous texture to dishes like the Poached Pears in Ginger Syrup (page 144). The recipe below can be used as a base – I have added almonds, but you can use any nut or spice you feel matches your dish; I would use ground ginger if I was making it for the pears.

*50g **gluten-free** oats*
*125g **gluten-free** plain flour*
50g demerara sugar
75g unsalted butter, cold
pinch of sea salt
50g chopped almonds (optional)

Preheat the oven to 180°C/160°C Fan/Gas Mark 4.

Place all the ingredients except the nuts in a large bowl and gently rub in the butter until you have a breadcrumb-like texture. Mix in the nuts, if using.

Transfer the mixture to a baking sheet and shake so the sheet is evenly covered. Place in the oven and cook for 10–12 minutes, then, using a fork, gently mix up the crumble, breaking up any large lumps. If it is a little brown around the edges, just work this into the rest of the mixture.

Return to the oven for 8–10 minutes, until it is a dark golden colour. Remove from the oven and leave to cool, then place in a sealed container for up to 48 hours.

hassle free, gluten free

Golden Syrup and Ginger Microwave-Steamed Sponge Pudding

serves 4–6

I often need to cook a last-minute dessert if the children have brought friends home, or if I am just not organised, so microwave-steamed sponge puddings are perfect. I sometimes use jams or frozen fruit, but this one is also a real favourite at home.

100g golden syrup
1 tablespoon lemon juice
125g unsalted butter, plus extra
 for greasing
125g soft brown sugar
2 large eggs
*125g **gluten-free** plain flour*
1 tablespoon ground ginger
1 teaspoon mixed spice

You will need
a 2lb glass or ceramic pudding basin

Liberally grease the pudding basin with butter. Put the golden syrup and lemon juice into the basin and mix together, then set the bowl aside.

Using an electric whisk, cream the butter and sugar together in a bowl until light and airy. Add the eggs one at a time, making sure to incorporate them properly; the mixture should be mousse-like.

Sift the flour and spices into the mixture in 3–4 batches, mixing carefully to keep the air in.

Put the batter into the basin on top of the golden syrup. Cover the bowl with clingfilm so it is well sealed, but still a little loose on top, and place in a microwave for 6 minutes on high.

Remove from the microwave and leave to stand for 5 minutes, then carefully tip out on to a plate. Serve immediately with lots of cream or custard.

Blackcurrant Polenta Cake

serves 12

Blackcurrants are one of my favourite fruits. My parents grow loads of them every year, and my mum patiently picks the top stalks off and freezes the berries to make jams and puddings throughout the year. It really is a labour of love. I've used frozen berries here – they taste amazing and are a lot easier.

450g frozen blackcurrants
4 tablespoons blackcurrant cassis (you can use a different alcohol, or simply water for a child-friendly version)
250g golden caster sugar, plus an extra 4 tablespoons
250g butter, softened, plus extra for greasing
○ *200g fine polenta*
150g ground almonds
*1½ teaspoons **gluten-free** baking powder*
3 large eggs

You will need
a 21cm square cake tin

Preheat the oven to 190°C/170°C Fan/Gas Mark 5. Grease the cake tin with butter and line with baking parchment.

Place the blackcurrants, cassis (or water) and 4 tablespoons of sugar in a pan and gently warm through until the sugar has dissolved, then remove from the heat. Set aside about 50g of the blackcurrants and add the rest to the base of the tin.

Put the 250g caster sugar, the butter, polenta, ground almonds, baking powder and eggs into a large mixing bowl and combine to create a thick batter. Carefully spoon on top of the blackcurrants and smooth over until even.

Place in the oven for 40 minutes, then remove and leave to cool in the tin. Once cool, turn the tin upside down onto a large plate, slice and serve with the reserved blackcurrants.

Fig and Orange
Polenta Cakes

These quick and easy polenta cakes make a lovely dessert and are a little different. They are not the same as a tarte tatin, but that's where the inspiration comes from and they are certainly delicious. Be warned: they need to be removed from the tins with care as they are fragile and very light; I take them out when they're warm with a small palette knife or dessertspoon.

6 figs
75g softened butter
75g caster sugar
1 large egg
○ 75g fine polenta
25g ground almonds
½ teaspoon **gluten-free** baking powder
50g natural yogurt
2 tablespoons freshly squeezed orange juice
grated zest of 1 small orange, plus extra to garnish

For the caramel
100g caster sugar
25g butter

For the boozy whipped cream
50ml double cream
1 teaspoon caster sugar
1 teaspoon Grand Marnier or Cointreau

Preheat the oven to 190°C/170°C Fan/Gas Mark 5.

To make the caramel, add the caster sugar to a heavy-based pan with a splash of water. Heat slowly, swirling the pan occasionally; do not stir, just keep over a steady heat until the sugar goes a dark golden caramel colour. Remove from the heat and quickly stir in the butter using a spatula or wooden spoon. It will froth a little so please be careful.

Gently and carefully pour equal portions of the caramel into six holes of a non-stick muffin tin.

Cut a cross in the top of each of the figs and push down a little so the tops open like flowers. Put flower-side-down into the prepared caramel tins.

Beat the softened butter and sugar with an electric whisk until really light and fluffy, then beat in the egg until the mixture is mousse-like and light in texture.

Add the polenta, ground almonds, baking powder, yogurt, orange juice and zest and beat with the electric whisk or a hand whisk to combine, then add to the holes of the muffin tin over the fig and caramel – you should need just over a dessertspoon of mixture per fig.

Place in the oven for 15–18 minutes, until light and golden. Leave to cool for a couple of minutes, then use a palette knife or dessertspoon to gently ease them out and place them on a board to cool for another 5 minutes.

For the cream, whip the cream and caster sugar until you have soft peaks, then add the liqueur to taste.

Serve warm with a spoonful of cream and sprinkled with a little grated orange zest.

Poached Pears
in **Ginger Syrup**

serves 6

This is my mum's favourite dessert. It is easy to make and can be kept in the fridge in the syrup for 3–4 days, so is ideal at Christmas time. I made a version of this dish in the second round of MasterChef, when you cook for the past contestants, so it has a special place in my heart. The pears are delicious served with Chantilly cream, which can also be prepared in advance.

2 cinnamon sticks
4 star anise
500ml ginger wine
1 x 350g jar of stem ginger in syrup
*6 ripe (not over-ripe) Conference
  pears*
2–3 tablespoons cooking brandy
1–2 tablespoons lemon juice
Chantilly cream, to serve

Put the cinnamon sticks, star anise, ginger wine and the whole jar of ginger and syrup into a large stock pot. Add 1 litre of water, but don't put over the heat.

Peel the pears carefully; I find this easier to do using a vegetable peeler. Leave the stalk on the top for decorative purposes. Using a melon baller (or I find the ½ teaspoon of my metal measuring spoons is a perfect size), gently remove the core from the centre of the pear, going in from the bottom and being careful not to break the pears. Drop the pears into the syrup mixture immediately to prevent browning.

Once all the pears are peeled and cored, put the pan over a low heat and simmer for 10–15 minutes, turning the pears to ensure even cooking. To test whether they are cooked, gently pierce the pears in the cored inside with a cocktail stick: they need to be firm enough to stand up but easily cut with a spoon.

Remove the pears gently using a slotted spoon and set aside. Turn up the heat and reduce the syrup until it coats the back of a spoon and leaves a path when you run your finger through it (carefully). The syrup needs to be thick enough to coat the pears and create a nice sauce in the dish when served.

Once the syrup has reduced, remove from the heat and strain, then add the brandy and lemon juice to taste.

Once the pears have cooled, cut the bottom off each one and stand them on individual plates. Liberally cover with the syrup and put a large spoon of Chantilly cream to the side. I prefer to serve these warm, so if you are making them a few days in advance I generally cover them in syrup and reheat them in the microwave for 2 minutes before serving.

hassle free, gluten free

Blackberry and Sloe Gin Semifreddo

serves 8–10

I have never owned an ice cream maker – they were always too expensive and took up too much room – however I do like to serve frozen desserts, as they can be prepared weeks in advance and pulled out of the freezer in an emergency (when I forget or am too busy to make pudding). I also make them in silicone cupcake moulds, freeze them and store them in sealed sandwich bags for a quick pud. This recipe might seem complicated, but I find the secret is to prep everything before you start, so you can move easily and quickly from one process to the next. I like the brambly dry flavour of the sloe gin with the blackberries, but if you prefer something sweeter use kirsch, or water will work for a child-friendly version.

450ml double cream
3 large egg yolks
4 tablespoons golden caster sugar

For the purée
600g frozen or fresh blackberries
125ml sloe gin
40g caster sugar

Prepare a bowl of iced water and set aside in the fridge. Pour the cream into a second bowl and keep in the fridge until needed. Line a 2lb loaf tin with baking parchment.

For the purée, place half the blackberries into a saucepan with the sloe gin and sugar. Simmer gently over a low heat for 3–5 minutes, until the sugar is dissolved and the blackberries are thawed (if using frozen). Use a stick blender, or mash the mixture into a purée and pass through a sieve to remove any pips. Place the purée into the fridge to chill.

Find a large bowl that fits comfortably into a saucepan without touching the bottom of the pan, then add some water to the pan – not so much that it touches the bottom of the bowl – and bring to the boil.

Once the water is boiling, put the egg yolks and sugar into the bowl and whisk by hand or with an electric whisk; you will quickly see the egg yolks change colour and consistency. Keep whisking until light in colour and fluffy. Once it has reached ribbon stage – when the whisk makes ribbons in the mixture that don't immediately disappear – carefully transfer the bowl into the bowl of iced water and continue whisking until the temperature of the mixture has been brought down to room temperature. Set aside.

Quickly wash the whisk, then take the cream from the fridge and whisk it to stiff peaks.

hassle free, gluten free

Add a large tablespoon of the cream to the egg yolk mixture and combine using a silicone spatula, if you have one. You need to keep as much air in the mix as possible, so use figure-of-eight movements and work as quickly as you can. Keep adding the cream in this way until about half is combined, then you can add the remainder and mix through.

Take 4 tablespoons of the purée and gently fold through the mixture in two or three quick actions; I like the mix to be marbled in effect. Carefully pour the semifreddo mix into the lined tin; it will come about two-thirds of the way up the sides. Place some clingfilm directly on top of the semifreddo so it is in contact with the surface, then wrap the tin in clingfilm and place the whole thing in the freezer. Alternatively, split equally among the holes of a 12-hole silicone bun tin.

Freeze for 2–3 hours, or overnight, until solid. Remove from the tin, place in a large freezer bag with the smaller bag of purée and the remaining blackberries and leave until needed. To serve, warm through the purée to defrost, and set aside the blackberries to defrost too. The semifreddo can be served straight from the freezer.

My Tip
If the semifreddo is difficult to remove from the tin, gently lower it into very hot water for a few seconds and it should then come away easily; don't leave it too long, though, or it will start to melt.

cakes, muffins and pancakes

Ginger Traybake with **Preserved Ginger** and **Lemon Icing**

serves 8–10

I use an electric hand whisk to make this cake, but a good old-fashioned wooden spoon and elbow grease work just as well. For the syrup and stem ginger listed in the ingredients you will need a 310g jar of stem ginger in syrup.

200g softened unsalted butter
200g soft dark brown sugar
3 large eggs
*200g **gluten-free** plain flour*
*2 teaspoons **gluten-free** baking powder*
1 tablespoon ground ginger
½ teaspoon sea salt
6 balls of stem ginger from a jar, chopped
2 tablespoons of the ginger syrup from a jar

For the icing
250g icing sugar
5 tablespoons lemon juice
2 tablespoons ginger syrup from a jar
2 balls of stem ginger from a jar, chopped
grated lemon zest (optional), to decorate.

You will need
a 22cm square cake tin

Preheat the oven to 180°C/160°C Fan/Gas Mark 4. Grease the tin with butter and line with greaseproof paper.

Cream the butter and sugar together in a bowl until light and fluffy. Add the eggs one by one; if the mixture starts to curdle, add a tablespoon of the flour into it and continue beating.

Combine the flour, baking powder, ground ginger and salt in a separate bowl.

Add the dry ingredients to the butter mixture in 3–4 batches, sifting it in from high up to get as much air into the cake as possible, then fold in using a spatula or spoon. Add the chopped ginger and ginger syrup and fold these into the cake mixture.

Transfer the mixture to the cake tin and smooth the top. Place on the middle shelf of the oven for about 20 minutes, until raised and cooked through when pierced with a skewer.

Remove from the oven and make the icing while the cake is cooling. Sift the icing sugar into a large bowl. Combine the lemon juice and ginger syrup and add to the icing sugar. The icing should be a little runny, not stiff, so you may need to adjust the quantities slightly to achieve this. Pour the icing over the cake while it's still in the tin. I like to ice this cake when warm so the icing melts into the cake a little. Dice the stem ginger and sprinkle over the top of the cake with a little lemon zest, if using.

Leave the cake to cool, then remove from the tin, discard the greaseproof paper, and cut the cake into squares.

Rhubarb and Pistachio Polenta Cake

serves 8–10

I love the colours and flavour combinations in this cake – it's surprisingly light and summery. You will get some dark areas around the edges from the sugars in the rhubarb, but I think this just adds to the overall effect. I love to make the syrup to pour over the top of the cake, but the cake also works well without it.

350g rhubarb, chopped into 1.5cm pieces
250g caster sugar, plus 1 tablespoon for the rhubarb
250g unsalted butter, softened, plus a little extra for greasing the tin
3 large eggs
○ 200g fine polenta
150g ground almonds, plus extra for lining the tin
grated zest of 1 medium orange
1½ teaspoons **gluten-free** baking powder
125g pistachios, roughly chopped

For the orange syrup (optional)
juice from the zested orange (see above)
1 tablespoon caster sugar

You will need
a 22cm round springform cake tin

Preheat the oven to 190°C/170°C Fan/Gas Mark 5. Grease the tin with butter, and line it with a sprinkling of the ground almonds.

Put the rhubarb pieces on a very lightly oiled baking tray and sprinkle with 1 tablespoon caster sugar. Place in the oven for 15 minutes, or until the rhubarb is tender but still holding its shape. Set aside and allow to cool.

Cream the butter and sugar together in a bowl with an electric whisk, then add the eggs one at a time.

My Tip
You could make the cake in a food processor, but I prefer to use an electric whisk or to do it by hand, as the rhubarb and pistachios need to be carefully folded in.

Add the polenta, ground almonds, orange zest and baking powder and mix in thoroughly.

Gently fold in three-quarters of the cooked rhubarb and pistachio nuts, reserving some for the top of the cake.

Put the mixture into the prepared tin, sprinkle over the remaining rhubarb and pistachios and place in the oven for 40–50 minutes, or until risen and golden.

While the cake is cooking, make the syrup, if using. Put the orange juice and sugar into a saucepan and bring to the boil, then reduce the heat to simmer and, without stirring which will form crystals, gently agitate the pan over the low heat until the liquid is reduced to a syrup. The sugar will just start to change colour. Pour this evenly over the cake while the cake is still warm from the oven, leave for 10 minutes in the tin, then remove and serve when ready.

Apricot and Almond Polenta Cake

serves 6–8

I often use canned and frozen fruit, I think they are a real store-cupboard standby. This cake looks beautiful and is very quick and easy to put together.

1 x 400g can of apricot halves
  in natural juice
150g butter, at room temperature,
  plus extra for greasing
100g golden caster sugar, plus extra
  for dusting
2 large eggs, separated
○ 100g fine polenta
○ 100g ground almond flour, plus
  extra for dusting
2 teaspoons mixed spice
1 teaspoon **gluten-free**
  baking powder
1 tablespoon black treacle
few drops of almond essence
25g flaked almonds

You will need
a 23cm springform cake tin

Preheat the oven to 190°C/170°C Fan/Gas Mark 5. Grease the cake tin with butter, and dust the tin with a little almond flour or line using greaseproof paper.

Drain and roughly chop all but 7 of the apricot halves that are equal in shape.

Cream together the butter and sugar in a bowl until light and fluffy, then add the egg yolks one at a time, and keep beating until well combined, light and fluffy.

Add the polenta, almond flour, mixed spice, baking powder, black treacle and almond essence to the bowl and beat in until completely combined.

Whisk the egg whites until stiff and glossy, and gently fold the cake mixture into the egg whites, a spoon at a time, retaining as much air as possible. Fold in until completely combined and there are no lumps.

Add the chopped apricots and fold evenly through the mixture.

Place the mixture into the tin and smooth the top with a spatula. Arrange the remaining apricot halves in a clock-face pattern on the top of the cake with one in the middle. Sprinkle over the flaked almonds, avoiding the apricot halves, and a little sugar.

Place on the middle shelf of the oven and bake for 40–45 minutes, until the cake is risen and golden. You can test it by piercing it with a cocktail stick – if it comes away dry, the cake is cooked.

Allow to cool and then remove from the tin. You can serve it warm or cold; it's lovely on its own or with a spoon of double cream or crème fraîche.

Movie Night
Brownies

serves 6–8,
depending on
the size of your
teenagers

I cook this brownie when we have a house full of teenagers; it saves on washing up and mess and they love the fact it comes in the pan, complete with fruit, ice cream or whatever else they put on it. Alternatively, you can cook it in a traditional tin and cut it into squares, if you prefer.

2 x 85g **gluten-free** chocolate,
   70 per cent cocoa solids, chopped
   (see Tip)
200g unsalted butter, cut into small
   cubes, plus extra for greasing
4 large eggs
225g caster sugar
125g **gluten-free** plain flour
pinch of sea salt
100g macadamia nuts, roughly
   chopped
85g **gluten-free** milk, white or
   mixed chocolate chips
○ 50g mini marshmallows

To serve (optional):
○ ice cream, chocolate or raspberry
   sauce, fresh fruit, salted popcorn,
   sprinkles – whatever takes
   your fancy

You will need
a 28cm ovenproof frying pan

Preheat the oven to 180°C/160°C Fan/Gas Mark 4. Generously grease the frying pan with a little butter.

Put the dark chocolate pieces and butter into a bowl set over a pan of simmering water. Once melted, remove from the heat and set aside to cool.

My Tip
I used raspberry-flavoured dark chocolate for this recipe, but salted caramel, coconut and ginger work really well too; use whatever is your favourite to add a little extra flavour.

Whisk the eggs and sugar together until really light and creamy and doubled in volume.

Gently fold the cooled chocolate and butter mixture into the eggs and sugar. Sift in the plain flour and salt and gently fold in.

Add the chopped macadamia nuts, chocolate chips and marshmallows to the mixture and pour into the frying pan, making sure the mixture is spread out evenly.

Place in the oven and cook for 20–25 minutes, until there is a crust on top but the insides are still a bit gooey.

Leave to cool in the pan and decorate as desired. We like to eat this a little warm, but cold is good too. Give everyone a spoon and put the movie on.

Traditional
Fairy Cakes

makes 12

This recipe is the same one I learnt from my nan and then passed on to my children when they were starting to bake. The mix makes twelve perfect fairy cakes – and if you double up they're perfect for bake sales at school. I have included a couple of my favourite flavours, but it's a blank canvas so go wild.

2 large eggs, weighed
depending on the weight of the eggs,
  you need the exact same weight of:
  unsalted butter
  softened golden caster sugar
  gluten-free *plain flour*
*1 teaspoon **gluten-free***
  baking powder

Preheat the oven to 200°C/180°C Fan/Gas Mark 6. Line a 12-hole bun tin with fairy cake cases.

Cream the butter and sugar together in a bowl with an electric whisk or by hand until soft and light. Add the eggs one at a time and beat in carefully until light and mousse-like.

Sift the flour and baking powder and add to the mixture in 3–4 batches. I use an electric whisk now for speed, as I am usually baking large quantities, but the old-fashioned method might give slightly better results.

Split the mixture equally between the fairy cake cases and bake for 20–25 minutes until risen and golden.

My Tip
When baking cakes, please be very careful not to over-soften the butter (in the microwave, for example) as it will become oily and really affect your sponge, making it denser and greasier. It's always slightly harder to get good results with gluten-free baking, and a simple thing like this can trip you up at the start of the process. Leave the butter to warm to room temperature on its own.

traditional fairy cake mix
    (see page 158)
zest of 1 lemon
zest of 1 orange

For the icing
juice of 1 lemon
juice of 1 orange
1 tablespoon caster sugar
1 tablespoon limoncello or orange
    liqueur (optional)
100g butter, softened
250g icing sugar

traditional fairy cake mix
    (see page 158)
○ 2 tablespoons cocoa powder
chocolates, to decorate

For the icing
150g butter, softened
50g cocoa powder
200g icing sugar

St Clements Fairy Cakes

Once the flour and baking powder are incorporated as above, add the lemon and orange zests to the mix and bake as directed.

For the icing, add the lemon and orange juice to a small saucepan with the caster sugar, and reduce down rapidly until you have about 2 tablespoons of syrupy liquid. Watch this carefully as it burns easily. Set aside to cool. (For an adult version, add a tablespoon of limoncello or orange liqueur to the icing at the end.)

Beat the softened butter with an electric hand whisk for a minute or two until light and airy, then carefully sift the icing sugar into the butter and whisk to incorporate, then repeat with another 125g icing sugar. Beat in the cooled syrup and spoon or pipe on to the cakes.

Chocolate Fairy Cakes

When weighing out the basic ingredients, replace 2 tablespoons of the flour with 2 tablespoons of cocoa powder, then follow the recipe given.

For the icing, beat the softened butter with an electric hand whisk for a minute or two until light and airy. Combine the cocoa powder with the icing sugar, then sift half of this mixture into the butter and whisk in. Once incorporated, repeat with the remaining icing sugar/cocoa mixture. If the icing is looking grainy, add a little water, half a teaspoon at a time, until it's smooth but still holds its shape.

I like to buy a couple of packets of the children's favourite hard chocolates to add to the icing. I smash the contents of one packet with a rolling pin, or put it in the food processor for 30 seconds, and keep the other one to decorate. Daim Bars are great for this, especially as they're gluten free. Mix the blitzed sweets into the icing, then pipe or spoon onto the cakes. Decorate with the second packet of chocolates.

Mince Pies

makes 12

I make this mincemeat and use it as soon as it has cooled down – it's just part of the Christmas preparation for me. The butter is there to add to the richness of the mincemeat, as suet would be added in a traditional recipe, but please feel free to leave it out if you feel it's unnecessary. I use a 12-hole muffin tin for deep-filled mince pies; if you prefer the more traditional thinner pie you can make 24.

1 x quantity Sweet Shortcrust
   Pastry (page 194)
1 egg, beaten, for egg wash

For the mincemeat
250ml brandy
75g demerara sugar
100g currants
100g sultanas
50g mixed peel
50g mixed dried cherries and
   berries (if not available, add extra
   currants and sultanas)
1 tablespoon lemon juice
50g freshly grated Granny
   Smith apple
25g warm butter

You will need
a 12-hole muffin tin; 9cm and 6cm
   ring cutters

For the mincemeat, place the brandy, 250ml water, sugar, dried fruit and lemon juice in a saucepan and bring to the boil. Reduce the heat and simmer for 30–40 minutes until all the liquid has nearly gone and you are left with fruit with the consistency of mincemeat.

Grate in the apple and stir through with the butter, then remove from the heat and chill to room temperature.

Preheat the oven to 200°C/180°C Fan/Gas Mark 6. Roll out the pastry to the thickness of a £1 coin. Cut out twelve 9cm rounds and line the holes of the tin, making sure there are no gaps (you can patch up gluten-free pastry, however, as it is quite forgiving).

Add 1 level dessertspoon of mincemeat mixture to each pie base, then cut out twelve 6cm rings for the lids.

Egg wash the edges of the pastry in the tin and place on the lids. Egg wash the lids and put two small slits into each one.

Place in the preheated oven for 18–20 minutes, until golden. Note that gluten-free pastry is always blonder in colour than non-gluten-free pastry, so don't be tempted to overcook trying to achieve a golden finish.

Remove from the oven and leave to cool a little. These are best served warm with brandy butter or whipped cream.

To reheat if necessary, warm through in the oven at 180°C/160°C Fan/Gas Mark 4 for 5 minutes.

Antipasti Muffin

makes 6–8

I often have some spare salami or olives hanging around in the fridge, and I hate waste, so I tend to use them up in a frittata or a muffin, which Ben can take to school and the others can use for lunches. Feel free to use halloumi or goat's cheese too if you have those left over.

225g **gluten-free** plain flour
2 teaspoons **gluten-free** baking powder
½ teaspoon bicarbonate of soda
2 teaspoons sea salt
a few good grinds of black pepper
2 large eggs
225g natural yogurt
2 tablespoons sunflower oil
100g Milano salami, roughly chopped
100g mixed olives, stones removed, roughly chopped
1 x 200g pack feta cheese, cut into 12 pieces

Preheat the oven to 200°C/180°C Fan/Gas Mark 6, and line six holes of a standard muffin tray with tulip muffin cases, or eight holes with standard paper cases.

My tip
I use tulip muffin cases as I have teenage boys who want larger portions of food. If you are using standard muffin cases you will get at least eight muffins from the mix.

Sift the flour, baking powder, bicarbonate of soda, salt and black pepper into a large bowl.

In a separate bowl, combine the eggs, yogurt and oil, then add to the dry ingredients and fold in. Don't overwork the mixture at this stage.

Fold in the chopped salami and olives. Crumble two chunks of feta into the mixture and fold in.

Half fill the muffin cases with the mixture. Push one piece of feta into the centre of each muffin, then continue to fill each case until full. Crumble the last bits of feta evenly across the top of the muffins.

Cook for 18 minutes, until risen and golden.

Breakfast One-Pan Muffin

makes 6–8

I have to be honest, when Ben was first diagnosed he did not really like bread. I am not sure if that was because he knew it made him ill, or whether gluten-free bread was pretty revolting all those years ago, and I struggled to make a good loaf for a long time. So I started to develop different ways of presenting food using bread substitutes, and this muffin has become a firm favourite. It's easy to do and is one-pan cooking. It does require a frying pan that goes in the oven, although I'm sure a non-stick roasting tin could be used instead. The secret is to not make the mixture too thick, so it cooks through but the egg yolks remain runny.

25g butter
1 x 250g pack streaky bacon, chopped
200g mushrooms, chopped
225g **gluten-free** plain flour
2 teaspoons **gluten-free** baking powder
½ teaspoon bicarbonate of soda
2 teaspoons sea salt
a few good grinds of black pepper
8 large eggs
225g natural yogurt
2 tablespoons sunflower oil
3 **gluten-free** sausages or 6 **gluten-free** chipolatas (use your favourite brand), cooked and chopped

Preheat the oven to 200°C/180°C Fan/Gas Mark 6.

Melt a little butter in an ovenproof non-stick frying pan (or non-stick roasting tin) and fry the chopped bacon and mushrooms until the bacon is cooked through and crispy. Leave to cool in the frying pan with the cooking juices while you make the muffin mix.

Sift the flour, baking powder, bicarbonate of soda, salt and black pepper into a large bowl.

In a separate bowl, combine 2 eggs with the yogurt and oil, then add to the dry ingredients and fold in. Don't overwork the mixture.

Combine the bacon, mushrooms and cooked sausages into the muffin mix and spread evenly over the bottom of the frying pan or roasting tin. Using the back of a spoon, gently press six indents into the mixture and crack an egg into each.

My Tip
Feel free to experiment: add onions or herbs, but be careful with tomatoes as they are wet and will add liquid to the mixture.

Place in the oven and cook for 12–15 minutes, until the muffin mixture is cooked through but the egg yolks are still runny. Place the pan on the table and slice while hot.

Cheese and Pickle Savoury Muffins

makes 6–8

For so long we struggled with lunches for Ben. He used to take gluten-free pasta every day, as he had a real problem with eating gluten-free bread. So I had to be creative with his lunchbox, and find something that was as easy to eat as a sandwich, and looked the same as what the other children were eating. Somewhere along the line the muffin became my friend – I use it to carry flavour in much the same way sandwiches do.

225g **gluten-free** *plain flour*
2 teaspoons **gluten-free**
  baking powder
½ *teaspoon bicarbonate of soda*
2 *teaspoons sea salt*
2 *large eggs*
225g *natural yogurt*
2 *tablespoons sunflower oil*
150g *mature Cheddar cheese, grated,*
  plus a little extra for sprinkling
  on top
○ 4 *tablespoons chunky pickle of*
  your choice

Preheat the oven to 200°C/180°C Fan/Gas Mark 6, and line six or eight holes of a standard muffin tray with your chosen cases (see Tip, page 164).

Sift the flour, baking powder, bicarbonate of soda and salt into a large bowl.

Combine the eggs, yogurt and oil in a separate bowl, then add these to the dry ingredients and fold in. Don't overwork the mixture at this stage.

Add the grated cheese and pickle to the mix and stir in gently.

Divide the mixture equally between the muffin cases, sprinkle a little extra cheese over the top of each muffin and place in the oven. Cook for 20–25 minutes, until golden on top.

Banana and Choc Chip Muffins

makes 6–8

Like most households, we go through fads with fruit – one week everyone is moaning that there are no bananas; the next week the bananas are going slowly black in the bowl as everyone has moved on to apples. Bananas and custard is always a favourite, but we also love these muffins as they are so quick and easy to knock up, and when teenagers are running late they can double up with some fruit as breakfast on the bus.

225g **gluten-free** *plain flour*
2 teaspoons **gluten-free**
  baking powder
½ teaspoon bicarbonate of soda
3 tablespoons golden caster sugar
1 teaspoon mixed spice
½ teaspoon sea salt
2 large eggs
225g natural yogurt
1 tablespoon sunflower oil
2 ripe bananas, mashed roughly
  with a fork
100g **gluten-free** *milk*
  chocolate chips
demerara sugar, for sprinkling

Preheat the oven to 200°C/180°C Fan/Gas Mark 6, and line six or eight holes of a standard muffin tray with your chosen cases (see Tip, page 164).

Sift the flour, baking powder, bicarbonate of soda, caster sugar, mixed spice and salt into a large bowl.

In a separate bowl, combine the eggs, yogurt and oil, then add to the dry ingredients and fold in. Don't overwork the mixture at this stage. Add the mashed banana and chocolate chips to the mix, and stir to combine.

Fill each muffin case evenly with the mixture and sprinkle with a little demerara sugar. Cook for 18–20 minutes, until risen and golden brown.

Maple Syrup and Bacon Muffins with Cream Cheese and Maple Syrup Topping

serves 6–8

I think these are my family's favourite muffins. I don't have a particularly sweet tooth but even I devour these when they are made.

225g **gluten-free** plain flour
2 teaspoons **gluten-free**
  baking powder
½ teaspoon bicarbonate of soda
2 tablespoons caster sugar
½ teaspoon sea salt
2 large eggs
225g natural yogurt
2 tablespoons sunflower oil
250g streaky bacon, fried until
  crispy, then chopped
1 tablespoon maple syrup

For the topping
250g cream cheese
4 tablespoons maple syrup, plus
  a little extra for drizzling
25g icing sugar, sifted
pinch of sea salt

Preheat the oven to 200°C/180°C Fan/Gas Mark 6, and line six or eight holes of a standard muffin tray with your chosen cases (see Tip, page 164).

Sift the flour, baking powder, bicarbonate of soda, sugar and salt into a large bowl.

Combine the eggs, yogurt and oil in a separate bowl, then add the wet ingredients to the dry ingredients and fold in. Don't overwork the mixture at this stage.

Add most of the fried bacon (reserve about 2 tablespoons for the topping) and the maple syrup and fold in gently until evenly distributed throughout the mixture.

Fill the muffin cases with the mixture and cook for 18 minutes, until a skewer inserted into the centre comes away dry. Set aside to cool.

To make the topping, use an electric whisk to mix together the cream cheese, maple syrup, icing sugar and salt, until the mixture is thick enough to be piped.

Once the muffins are cool, pipe or spoon on the topping and sprinkle with the chopped bacon. Drizzle a little maple syrup over the top and serve.

Pancakes

makes 8–10
pancakes

I used to spend hours cooking these for four children and all of their friends on Pancake Day. Nowadays it's a little easier as I have fewer to cook for, but they still make a delicious, quick pud. As with everything, I find the easiest way to make these is to get prepped: I have a little bowl or jug of oil, my cold chopped butter and the batter to hand, with a ladle all ready to go. My favourite topping is lemon and sugar, but I lay out all sorts: ice cream, chocolate sauce, fruit sauce, maple syrup, soft fruits, sprinkles, and so on. The children then just make up their own, with some quite comical results!

225g **gluten-free** plain flour
250ml milk
2 large eggs
25g cold butter, cut into small
   chunks
sunflower oil

Put the flour, milk and eggs into a bowl or jug and whisk to combine until you have a thin, lump-free batter.

Heat a non-stick frying pan and add a little butter and a splash of oil, and swirl the pan to coat the base and sides.

Put two-thirds of a ladle of batter into the pan and quickly swirl around, cooking for a minute or two until golden brown on the underside. Flip the pancake using a palette knife, or toss the pancake. Repeat with the remaining butter, oil and batter; if the batter gets thicker towards the end, just add another splash of milk.

Serve with your favourite topping.

American-Style Pancakes

makes 7

Everyone loves pancakes, and my family are no exception. These fluffy American-style pancakes are perfect for breakfast – and for lunch and dinner too, according to my children.

200g **gluten-free** plain flour
1 teaspoon **gluten-free** baking powder
½ teaspoon sea salt
2 tablespoons caster sugar
100ml milk
1 large egg, separated
30g butter, melted, plus extra for cooking
splash of sunflower oil

Sift the flour, baking powder, salt and sugar together into a bowl. In a separate bowl, combine the milk, egg yolk and cooled melted butter, and in a third bowl, whisk the egg white with an electric whisk until stiff peaks form.

Beat the milk mixture into the flour mixture until a smooth but thick batter is achieved, then drop spoonfuls of the batter into the whisked egg white, carefully folding in to retain as much air as possible, and leave to stand for about 10 minutes.

Heat a non-stick frying pan with a knob of butter and a small splash of oil to stop the butter burning. Once the pan is hot, add dollops of the batter and gently flatten with the back of a spoon until they are your desired size – don't make them too thick. They won't be a perfect shape but they don't spread as evenly as traditional pancake batter mix. My pan can hold about two pancakes at a time.

Wait until the top of the pancake begins to bubble, then turn it over and cook until both sides are golden brown. Repeat until all the batter is used. These are best served straight from the pan, but you can put them into a warm oven until you finish cooking them all.

Mini Doughnuts Dusted with Cinnamon Sugar

My friend and fellow MasterChef contestant Juanita Hennessey makes the most delightful goat's cheese beignets with honey, and with her kind permission I have made a few adjustments to her recipe and created these little doughnuts or beignets. They are a little fiddly to make, but so very well worth the effort!

100g unsalted butter
20g golden caster sugar
*150g **gluten-free** plain flour*
1 teaspoon xanthan gum
pinch of sea salt
4 large eggs, beaten
sunflower oil, for frying

For the sugar
1 tablespoon ground cinnamon
4 tablespoons golden caster sugar

Put the butter, 300ml water and sugar into a large saucepan and bring to the boil, making sure all the butter has melted. Once boiling, turn the heat down to a simmer.

Sift the flour, xanthan gum and salt into a bowl, then add to the water and butter mixture. Beat well with a wooden spoon until you have a ball of smooth paste; this will go lumpy to begin with but do persevere. Remove from the heat and place on a steady surface.

Slowly add the eggs in 5–6 batches. I use an electric whisk, but your wooden spoon and muscles will do the work too. After you have added a little egg, beat or whisk until all of it is incorporated. If using an electric whisk, the mixture will creep up the whisks – just use a spoon and push it back down. Once all the egg is incorporated you will have a smooth, sticky, thick batter.

Fill a heavy-based pan one-third full with oil and heat to a temperature of 180°C. If you don't have a thermometer, simply drop a little of the batter into the pan; if it sinks then rises, sizzling, your oil is hot enough.

For the sugar, combine the cinnamon and sugar in a bowl. Prepare a clean tray and sprinkle a layer of cinnamon sugar over it.

Drop a small spoonful of the mixture into the oil. Don't overload the pan or the temperature of the oil will drop – I cook them in batches of six. Fry for 5–6 minutes, turning halfway to get an even golden colour. Remove the doughnuts from the oil using a slotted spoon and shake off any excess oil. Gently place in the cinnamon sugar immediately and roll to coat.

Repeat the process until all the mixture has been used. These are best eaten immediately, although they can be warmed through in an oven and eaten later the same day.

breads and doughs

Basic Bread Recipe

makes 1 loaf

I have tried many gluten-free bread recipes but I finally threw away the rule book and started from scratch and created my own. First and foremost, it needed to have the best taste possible, as well as a crusty top and the structural integrity to be made into a sandwich. I am still adapting and changing the recipe but this is the one I use now; Ben loves it and it's very easy. I don't use gluten-free bread flour, just gluten-free plain flour.

*2 x 7g sachet **gluten-free** quick-dried yeast*
3 teaspoons caster sugar
260ml warm water
*400g **gluten-free** plain white flour*
2 teaspoons salt
2 teaspoons xanthan gum
2 egg yolks
90ml olive oil, plus extra for oiling the tin
2 teaspoons cider vinegar
4 large egg whites

You will need
a 2lb non-stick loaf tin

Add the yeast and sugar to the warm water and leave to stand for about 5 minutes. It should form a head like a pint of beer; if it doesn't your yeast may not be active so discard and start again.

Meanwhile sift the flour into a bowl, add the salt and xanthan gum and stir to combine. Add 1 of the egg yolks, the olive oil, cider vinegar and active yeast mixture to the flour and mix to form a stiff dough.

In a separate large bowl, whisk the egg whites to stiff glossy peaks.

Add a small tablespoon of the dough mixture to the whisked egg whites and whisk in until no lumps remain. I do this a couple of times and then start adding slightly larger amounts of the dough to the egg white and whisk with an electric hand whisk. You need to maintain as much air in the dough as possible. Once all the dough is incorporated you will have a mixture much wetter than a normal dough.

Lightly oil the tin with a little olive oil. Place the dough in the tin and, with damp hands, gently press to the edges and flatten the top. Set aside in a warm place for about 30–40 minutes to rise; this is temperature dependent so don't worry if it takes a little more time. It should rise about 1–2cm above the rim of the tin. I don't cover the loaf as I find this helps to get a nice crust to the loaf.

Meanwhile, preheat the oven to 190°C/170°C Fan/Gas Mark 5.

Carefully egg wash the top of the loaf using the remaining egg yolk; it will be wobbly so be gentle. Place in the oven for 40–45 minutes, until the top is light golden and crisp.

My Tip
I use a lot of egg whites in my recipes, but if you don't want to waste a whole egg you can buy pasteurised egg whites in a lot of supermarkets now. As a note, the average weight of a large egg white is 40g.

Focaccia

serves 4–6

This is my basic focaccia bread mix. I have added two of my favourite fillings on pages 184 and 185, but it really is a very versatile bread so feel free to use your imagination. This recipe results in great bread time after time.

7g sachet **gluten-free** fast-action
    dried yeast
1½ teaspoons caster sugar
130ml warm water
200g **gluten-free** plain white flour
1 teaspoon sea salt, plus extra
    for sprinkling
1 teaspoon xanthan gum
2 eggs, separated
3 tablespoons olive oil, plus extra for
    oiling the tin and drizzling
1 teaspoon cider vinegar
6 small sprigs of fresh rosemary

You will need
a non-stick 23cm springform tin

Add the yeast and sugar to the warm water and leave to stand for about 5 minutes. It should form a head like a pint of beer; if it doesn't, your yeast may not be active so discard and start again.

Meanwhile, sift the flour into a bowl, add the salt and xanthan gum and stir to combine. Add 1 egg yolk, the olive oil, cider vinegar and active yeast mixture to the flour and mix to form a soft dough.

In a separate large bowl, whisk the egg whites to stiff glossy peaks.

Add a small tablespoon of the dough mixture to the whisked egg whites and whisk in until no lumps remain. I do this a couple of times and then start adding larger amounts, 2 tablespoons at a time, to the egg whites, whisking with an electric hand whisk. We want to keep as much air in the mix as possible. Once all the dough is incorporated, you will have a mixture much wetter than a normal dough, hence the springform cake tin to keep its shape.

Lightly oil the tin with a little olive oil. Place the dough in the tin and, with damp hands, gently press to the edges. Set aside in a warm place covered with a slightly damp cloth for 1 hour to rise.

Once risen, preheat the oven to 190°C/170°C Fan/Gas Mark 5 and beat the remaining egg yolk. Egg wash the top of the dough, place the six sprigs of rosemary into the dough and sprinkle with sea salt.

Place in the oven for 20–25 minutes, until the top is light golden and crisp. Remove from the oven and drizzle lightly with olive oil. The bread is best served warm.

Left: wild garlic pesto
focaccia (page 184);
Right: tapas focaccia
(page 185)

Wild Garlic (or Watercress) Pesto Focaccia

serves 4–6

This is such a seasonal bread, and I am aware that not everyone has access to wild garlic, so I use watercress when I can't get hold of the garlic. However it does herald spring and that first sneaky barbecue of the year, so I had to include it in the book.

1x quantity focaccia dough
(see page 181)

For the pesto
100g wild garlic leaves (after washing and large stalks removed) or 100g watercress (after washing and large stalks removed)
25g whole blanched hazelnuts
10g Parmesan, grated
½ tablespoon lemon juice
2–3 tablespoons extra-virgin olive oil
pinch of sea salt

If using the wild garlic for the pesto, put the leaves into a large saucepan and pour on boiling water. Leave to sit for 30 seconds and drain immediately. Squeeze out any excess water – I use kitchen towel on top of the leaves in a colander, and push down to remove the water. If using watercress, it's fine to use it raw.

Put all the pesto ingredients into a food processor, or use a hand blender and whizz until the mixture forms a thick paste; you want this drier than a normal pesto, so that when it is added to the bread it does not cause the bread to become heavy and laden with oil.

For the bread, follow the recipe as on page 181. Once the dough and egg whites are combined, add 1½ tablespoons of pesto to the dough and fold in, then continue with the rest of the recipe as instructed, but without the addition of the rosemary sprigs.

My Tip
You will have some pesto left over; if you add a little more olive oil, lemon juice and salt, it's a wonderful dip for bread. I also use it to flavour gluten-free pasta or rice, or it's great with fish or lamb. If kept in the fridge in a sealed container, it will be fine for 3–4 days.

Tapas Focaccia

serves 4–6

This is the bread I make most in the summer. It's so easy, and great for barbecues and lunches. I often call it leftover bread, as any little bits of salami and olives or sundried tomatoes you have get thrown in and used up.

1x quantity focaccia dough
  (see page 181)
75g chopped pitted olives (a mix
  of black and green, or whatever
  you prefer)
30g sliced salami, chopped
30g sliced chorizo, chopped

For the bread, follow the recipe as on page 181. Once the dough and egg whites are combined, add the olives, salami and chorizo to the mixture, then continue with the rest of the recipe as instructed, but without the addition of the rosemary sprigs.

Fondue Bread

serves 6 as a
sharing starter

This bread is fabulous to serve as a starter or as part of a lunch for a large group of people to tear and share. When you cut into it the cheese just runs out.

sunflower oil, for greasing the tin
1 x 250g Brie, Camembert or
    similar cheese; Tunworth is my
    local cheese and my favourite to use
    in this recipe
1 x 75g pack of Parma or Serrano
    ham (about 6 thin slices)
2 x quantities focaccia dough
    (page 181)
1 egg yolk, beaten, to egg wash

You will need
a 23cm round, 15cm deep
    springform tin

Lightly oil the springform tin.

Wrap the cheese wheel in the Parma ham slices so the cheese is encased.

Place about a third of the dough mixture into the base of the tin. Place the Parma ham-wrapped cheese into the centre and pile the rest of the dough on top. Don't worry – it will create a dome in the centre, but once risen it will surround the cheese. Leave to rest, covered, in a warm place for 2 hours, until the dough is risen and springy.

Preheat the oven to 190°C/170°C Fan/Gas Mark 5.

Use the egg yolk to egg wash the dough and place the tin in the oven for 45–50 minutes, until golden brown on top. If you're not sure it's cooked, release the spring and gently tap the side of the loaf – it should sound hollow.

Once cooked, remove from the oven and leave to cool for 10 minutes, then serve so the cheese is still lovely and runny.

Tear and Share Doughball Bread

serves 6–8

One of the best ways to eat these dough balls is with lashings of garlic butter, but I have also included halloumi and the little piquanté peppers from a jar. You can add any flavourings that take your fancy, really.

300ml warm milk
2 x 7g sachets **gluten-free** fast-action dried yeast
2 teaspoons caster sugar
375g **gluten-free** plain flour
1 tablespoon xanthan gum
2 teaspoons sea salt
1 teaspoon olive oil
1 egg, beaten, to egg wash

Additional flavours (optional)
1 x 225g pack halloumi, diced into 1cm cubes
100g mild piquanté peppers, from a jar, chopped

You will need
a 21cm round, 7cm deep spring form tin

In a bowl, combine the warm milk with the yeast and sugar and set aside for 5–10 minutes until a head has formed, similar to the froth on a pint of beer; if it doesn't form, your yeast may not be active, so discard and start again.

Weigh out the rest of the dry ingredients into a bowl. Once the milk and yeast mixture is ready, add it to the dry ingredients with the olive oil and combine to form a dough using an electric whisk. If the mixture is a little wet, add more flour. Add any additional flavours such as the halloumi and peppers now and incorporate into the dough.

Divide the dough into ten equal-sized pieces and roll each into a ball (roughly the size of a table tennis ball). Starting in the middle of the tin, place them around the tin so they form a flower shape. Set aside in a warm place for 45–60 minutes, until the dough has risen to the top of the tin.

Preheat the oven to 220°C/200°C Fan/Gas Mark 7, and egg wash the top of the risen dough.

Place in the oven for 45–60 minutes, until risen and golden. When you tap the bottom it should sound hollow. This is great served as part of a sharing platter or with soups.

Flat Breads

makes 4

These are very quick and easy to make. I know it's unusual to use yeast in a flat bread, but I find it gives the bread a lightness that is difficult to achieve otherwise – it does work!

150ml warm milk
1 teaspoon caster sugar
1 x 7g sachet **gluten-free** quick-action dried yeast
200g **gluten-free** plain flour
½ tablespoon xanthan gum
1 teaspoon sea salt
1 tablespoon olive oil

Combine the warm milk, sugar and yeast together in a bowl and leave for 5–8 minutes in a warm place for the yeast to become active. It should form a head like a pint of beer; if it doesn't, your yeast may not be active so discard and start again.

Sift the flour into a large bowl and add the xanthan gum and salt.

Once the yeast is active, add the milk mixture and the olive oil to the flour and use a spatula to combine. You can then use your hands to knead gently until you have a ball of dough and the mixture comes cleanly away from the sides. Cover with a slightly damp tea towel and leave to rest in a warm place for 15–30 minutes.

Cut the dough into four and roll out the flat breads to the size of pitta breads on a very lightly floured surface, or between two sheets of baking parchment to prevent the dough sticking to the worktop.

Heat a non-stick frying pan until hot and gently place one of the breads in the pan. Try to keep the heat in the pan constant, as you don't want to burn the bread and it needs to cook evenly. Leave in the pan until dark golden brown dots appear on the underside, then flip over and cook the other side until it has a similar appearance and no wax-like spots can be seen.

Remove and repeat until all the flat breads are cooked. Serve warm with gluten-free dips, such as the Carrot and Parsnip Hummus (page 21) and Chickpea, Spinach and Basil Dip (page 20).

Pizza Dough with Tomato Sauce

makes 4 x
18–20cm
pizza bases

The recipe below is for the pizza bases and sauce. Before cooking, cover the sauce with mozzarella cheese and your chosen pizza toppings – I find pre-grated mozzarella works better than fresh, as it releases less liquid, but go with your own preference. There is also constant debate in our house over using pineapple as a pizza topping – my answer is no!

For the dough
600ml warm milk
4 teaspoons caster sugar
4 x 7g sachets **gluten-free** fast-action dried yeast
700g **gluten-free** plain flour, plus extra for dusting
2 tablespoons xanthan gum
4 teaspoons sea salt
4 tablespoons olive oil

For the tomato sauce
1 x 500g pack passata
2 tablespoons olive oil
2 tablespoons dried mixed herbs
pinch of sea salt

Combine the warm milk, sugar and yeast together in a bowl and leave for 5–8 minutes in a warm place for the yeast to become active. It should form a head like a pint of beer; if it doesn't, your yeast may not be active so discard and start again.

Sift the flour into a large bowl and add the xanthan gum and salt.

Once the yeast is active, add the milk mixture and the olive oil to the flour and use a spatula to combine. You can then use your hands to knead gently until a ball of dough is in the bowl and the mixture comes cleanly away from the sides. Leave in the bowl to prove in a warm place for around 30–45 minutes. The dough should have doubled in size and be soft and springy to the touch.

Meanwhile, make the sauce. Put all the ingredients into a pan and simmer over a low heat for 5–10 minutes until you have a thick sauce. Take care, as the sauce spits while cooking.

Preheat the oven to 220°C/200°C Fan/Gas Mark 7.

Cut the dough into four equal pieces. Lightly dust one piece of dough in flour and roll out. The edges will be a little ragged, but just push them back in and round them off as you go to neaten them up. Repeat with the remaining pieces of dough – each quarter should stretch to form an 18–20cm pizza base.

Spread the cooked sauce evenly over each base, then add mozzarella and your chosen toppings and pop into the oven for 15 minutes. I cook mine on a pizza stone, but a baking sheet would also work.

Yorkshire Puddings

makes 18

I cook these when I have taken the roast out of the oven; this gives the meat time to rest and I can make sure the Yorkshires are cooked to perfection and the last thing to go on the plate. They are a little lighter than regular Yorkshire puddings, but still taste delicious. If you have any left over (not a regular occurrence), my grandad used to eat them with golden syrup and cream.

*175g **gluten-free** plain flour*
*1 teaspoon **gluten-free***
baking powder
½ teaspoon xanthan gum
pinch of sea salt
6 large eggs
450ml cold semi-skimmed or
full-fat milk
sunflower oil (or ideally the fat from
a cooked roast)

Sift the flour, baking powder, xantham gum and salt into a large bowl. In a separate bowl or jug, add the eggs and milk and beat or whisk together, then slowly beat the milk and egg mixture into the sifted flour until you have a smooth batter.

Transfer to a jug at this stage and place in the fridge for an hour, if you have the time; cold batter will help the Yorkshires to rise.

Preheat the oven to 220°C/200°C Fan/Gas Mark 7, or adjust the temperature if you have just taken your roast out. Put a little of the fat from the roast, or a little sunflower oil, into the holes of a non-stick muffin tin (you may need two tins) and place the tin(s) in the oven to heat for a few minutes.

Carefully pour equal quantities of the mixture into the bubbling fat in the tin(s) and return to the oven for 25 minutes. Please resist the urge to open the oven door and have a look – keep the door shut!

My Tip
When adding the mixture to the hot fat, I pull out the tin on the oven shelf and pour the mixture straight from the jug so I don't have to lift the hot fat from the oven. It means I can work more quickly and the fat stays hot.

When the time is up, open the oven door to release the steam, then turn the oven down to 190°C/170°C Fan/Gas Mark 5, and cook for a further 5 minutes to set the Yorkshires.

Remove from the oven and serve immediately, if possible. Alternatively, you could cook them in advance and reheat in a warm oven, if necessary.

Shortcrust Pastry

makes 500g

For years I made my pastry by hand. I now have a food processor which does it instantly, however I really believe that when starting out it's best to do it by hand so you get a feel for how it comes together. Adding the water at the end is key: too much and the pastry will be sticky and hard, too little and it will be crumbly, so take your time with that last tablespoon.

Do note that gluten-free pastry will not colour in the same way as non-gluten-free pastry will, so be sure not to overcook it. Egg washing before cooking will help achieve colour too.

50g cornflour
250g **gluten-free** plain flour
1 teaspoon xanthan gum
pinch of sea salt
125g butter, straight from the
    fridge, cubed
1 large egg

Put the cornflour, flour, xanthan gum and salt in a large bowl with the cubed butter. Gently rub the butter into the flour using your fingertips until you have created a crumb.

Make a well in the centre and add the egg and 2 tablespoons of cold water. Use your fingers to stir the mixture and incorporate the egg and water. If it's still a little crumbly, add a little more water and gently bring the pastry dough together with your hand, kneading lightly until it forms a ball and comes away easily from the sides of the bowl.

My Tips
I use the pastry straight after making it; if you refrigerate it for too long, it will become hard and unusable.

I roll it between two sheets of baking parchment as it is stickier than usual. To use, I take the top sheet of paper off and just pick up the bottom sheet with the pastry on it and place it carefully into the tin, then I remove the other sheet. If the pastry tears, don't worry, it's so much easier to patch than regular pastry. Even if you have some small cracks in the pastry after blind baking, you can patch these with a little raw pastry.

Finally, I have found many differences depending on which flour I use. This recipe is my standard, but some flours need a little more or less water. The more water, the harder the pastry, so it's a careful balance!

Sweet Shortcrust Pastry
Add 2 teaspoons of icing sugar instead of the salt.

Cheese Shortcrust Pastry
Add 50g finely grated Parmesan to the dough after it's come together, and work it through.

Breadcrumbs and Sage and Onion Stuffing

serves 4–6

Wherever I have used polenta to coat something for frying in this book, you can also use these breadcrumbs instead. Gluten-free breadcrumbs are available in shops, however I make my own mainly because Ben often does not eat the bread I make or buy for him! If you have a food processor this will take minutes, but it can easily be done by hand too – it just takes a little more patience.

For the breadcrumbs
*stale white **gluten-free** bread,
    sliced and toasted to a light golden
    brown, then left to cool*

For the stuffing
*1 onion, finely chopped
    (approx. 200g)
90g butter, plus extra for greasing
1 tablespoon finely chopped
    fresh sage
100g **gluten-free** breadcrumbs
1 egg
sea salt and freshly ground
    black pepper*

To make the breadcrumbs, finely chop the toasted bread, or place it in a food processor and pulse until you have breadcrumbs. Set aside 100g for the stuffing, and freeze the remainder in a ziplock freezer bag, not packed too tightly, and just use handfuls in other recipes as required.

Grease an ovenproof dish with a little butter – my dish is 20 x 13 x 3.5cm – and preheat the oven to 200°C/180°C Fan/Gas Mark 6.

Put the onion and 75g of butter into a saucepan and sauté gently until just starting to turn golden brown. Add the chopped sage, a little salt and pepper and 100g gluten-free breadcrumbs, and stir through until all of the butter is absorbed. Check the seasoning and add more salt and pepper if required. Add 2 tablespoons of water and stir to combine.

Remove the pan from the heat. Beat the egg in a little bowl and stir through the mixture.

Place the stuffing into the buttered dish, press down gently, fluff up the top with a fork, and dot the rest of the butter over the stuffing mix. Place in the oven for 20–25 minutes, until golden brown on top.

salads, sides and sauces

Caramelised
Banana Shallots

serves 8

This is a sneaky cheat to help make these lovely shallots extra quickly. They look so fabulous on a plate – the perfect accompaniment to most meats – and taste really good too. I love them as they can be cooked in advance and reheated when needed, or just finished off in the pan last minute.

4 large banana shallots, unpeeled
large knob of butter
sprig of fresh thyme
sprinkle of caster sugar

Place the shallots in a large saucepan, covered with water, and bring to the boil. Reduce the heat and simmer for about 30 minutes, until the shallots can be pierced through easily with a cocktail stick. Drain and set aside to cool a little, or until you are ready to serve.

Cut the shallots in half from the root to the tip, then carefully peel off the skin. Leave the ends intact so the shallots hold their shape.

In a non-stick saucepan, melt the butter with the thyme.

Sprinkle the cut sides of the shallots lightly with the sugar and fry in the butter until dark golden and caramelised. Flip over and cook the base a little. Remove from the pan and plate immediately.

hassle free, gluten free

Creamed Shallots

serves 4–6
as a side dish

This recipe tastes delicious, particularly when paired with lamb. I have always hated peeling shallots and baby onions, but with this recipe I boil them in their skins and they literally pop out, making life so much easier – which is exactly what I want when I'm cooking. This is one recipe for which I try to find the packet with the smallest onions in it!

450g shallots
1 garlic clove
sprig of fresh thyme, plus a few extra
* leaves to serve*
25g butter
*100ml **gluten-free** chicken stock*
100ml double cream
sea salt and freshly ground
* black pepper*

Place the unpeeled shallots in a pan of water and bring to the boil. Simmer until the largest is easily pierced with a toothpick and cooked all the way through, about 5 minutes. Remove from the heat, drain and allow to cool until you can handle them easily.

Once cool, peel the shallots – they should just pop out of their skins – and place in a saucepan. Finely grate the garlic clove into the pan, add the thyme, butter and a little salt and pepper, and heat gently for a couple of minutes until the garlic is cooked and translucent. (This is when the kitchen smells heavenly and everyone asks what you are making.) Don't try to brown the onions, you just want to gently cook the garlic and thyme.

Add the chicken stock and bring rapidly to the boil, then reduce the heat to a simmer and add the double cream. Continue to boil for a couple of minutes until the cream turns thicker and goes a darker colour, like rice pudding. Remove from the heat, sprinkle with a few thyme leaves and serve.

Spinach, Garlic and **Chilli Roast** Tomato Salad

serves 4

This is a really versatile salad that can be served with any roast or barbecued meats. I like it with the Braised Garam Masala Shoulder of Lamb on page 84 for something a bit different.

300g cherry tomatoes, halved
2 tablespoons olive oil
3–4 garlic cloves, thinly sliced
1 red chilli, finely chopped
150g baby spinach
lemon juice, to taste
sea salt and freshly ground
*   black pepper*

Preheat the oven to 190°C/170°C Fan/Gas Mark 5. Place the halved cherry tomatoes in a roasting tin with the olive oil and a little salt and pepper.

Sprinkle over the garlic and chilli, and try to make sure they sit on top of the tomatoes to ensure they don't burn.

Place in the oven for 30 minutes, until the tomatoes are sticky and cooked. Remove from the oven and add the spinach to the roasting tin, quickly mixing it through the tomatoes to wilt.

Add salt and lemon juice to taste, and serve immediately.

Pepper Salad

serves 4–6
as a side dish

We love peppers and eat them raw and cooked, however it is one vegetable that I seem to find goes a little wrinkly in the bottom of the fridge. Rather than waste them I make this quick salad, which is so versatile, and can be added to dishes like the Spanish Omelette (page 47) or chopped up and served with the Lamb and Feta Sliders (page 77).

3–4 peppers, ideally red or yellow, finely sliced
2 tablespoons olive oil
2 tablespoons cider vinegar or white wine vinegar
1 teaspoon fresh or dried oregano, or dried mixed herbs
1–2 garlic cloves, minced
sea salt and freshly ground black pepper, to taste

Place all the ingredients in a saucepan, stir to coat, then put the lid on the pan and cook gently over a low heat for around 20 minutes, until very soft and tender.

You can eat these straight away, or allow to cool and place in a lidded container in the fridge. They will keep for 48 hours, and you can reheat as you need them.

Butterbean, Thyme and Garlic Stew

serves 4

This is a very simple recipe with beautiful results – I love the earthiness of this stew. It works well with lamb (just replace the pork ribs with lamb bones), but is a particular favourite when served with the Smoked Paprika-Marinated Belly of Pork on page 88.

*1 litre **gluten-free** chicken stock*
2 garlic cloves, very finely chopped
  or smashed
3–4 sprigs of fresh thyme
2 pork ribs (see page 88)
2 x 400g cans of butterbeans

Put the chicken stock into a saucepan with the garlic, thyme and two pork ribs (I get the butcher to chop mine in half so they fit in the pan; if not, use a frying pan) and gently simmer for 10 minutes.

Add the butterbeans to the stock and continue to simmer for about 15 minutes, until you have a lovely stew.

Spicy Chorizo Rice

serves 4–6
as a main dish
and up to 10 as
a side dish

This is one of our favourite recipes, and if ever we have a barbecue, or I'm doing a big spread, then I generally cook this rice. It's very versatile, you can shred in pork or chicken, or add extra seafood, and it's particularly nice with a small can of drained sweetcorn stirred through.

2 tablespoons olive oil
225g chorizo, diced
1 large onion, finely diced
2 garlic cloves, finely chopped
1½ teaspoons smoked paprika
1 red chilli, kept whole but sliced
  down the middle
450g basmati rice
500g passata
*1 **gluten-free** chicken stock cube*
1–2 tablespoons lemon juice, to taste
225g cooked king prawns (optional)
sea salt

Put the olive oil and chorizo in a large pan, with a lid; I use a stock pot or a large non-stick pan. Slowly fry the chorizo until it is starting to brown and crisp on the outside and has released its lovely orange oil, then remove from the pan with a slotted spoon and set aside.

Using the oil from the chorizo, fry the onion and garlic until the onion begins to soften, about 3–5 minutes. Add the paprika and chilli, then add the rice and stir until evenly coated in the orange oil.

My Tip

When using a chilli, I often leave it whole, with the top stalk attached, and slice through the middle lengthways. This way I can easily remove it when the dish is hot or spicy enough for me.

Pour in the passata and 500ml of water, add the stock cube and stir through. Bring to the boil then put the lid on and turn the heat down to a slow simmer. Cook for 12–15 minutes, or until the rice is cooked through. Add the chorizo back to the pan. Remove the chilli and stir through the lemon juice and a pinch of salt to taste.

If eating immediately, add the prawns and stir through, but if serving cold later, stir them through just before serving.

My Tip

If serving cold and the rice is stuck together, you can drizzle a little olive oil through to loosen the grains. Try not to over-stir the rice when warm as it can break down and become mushy.

Top left: egg fried rice
(page 206)
Bottom left: turmeric,
sultana and coconut
basmati rice (page 207);
Right: spicy chorizo rice
(page 203)

Egg Fried Rice

serves 4

I make this using leftover rice. Ben often takes a bowl for lunch or I serve it with quick stir-fries; the children particularly love it with the Chilli Pork Spare Ribs (page 87).

2–3 tablespoons sunflower oil
bunch of spring onions, chopped
75g chestnut or white mushrooms, chopped
2 garlic cloves, chopped
75g frozen peas, cooked
300–350g cooked basmati rice
1 large egg
2 tablespoons **gluten-free** soy sauce
sprinkle of sesame oil (optional)

Heat the oil in a non-stick frying pan, add the spring onions and mushrooms and cook until the onion is soft, even a little charred, then add the garlic and cook for a further 2–3 minutes.

Add the cooked peas, rice and egg. Using a spatula, stir the egg through the rice mixture. Don't allow it to burn, but make sure all of the egg is cooked and distributed through the rice.

Add soy sauce to taste, and sprinkle with sesame oil, if using.

My Tip
You can easily add other vegetables or leftover chicken, pork or prawns to the rice to make a more substantial meal.

Turmeric, Sultana and **Coconut** Basmati Rice

serves 4

I love the colour that turmeric brings to a dish – and it's supposed to be really good for you too. This rice goes beautifully with the Mutton Curry (page 75). I use 75g rice per person, but if you want larger portions, use 90g per person.

50g unsalted butter
2 teaspoons ground turmeric
300g basmati rice
750ml **gluten-free** stock (if serving with a lamb curry, I use lamb stock; if it's a chicken curry, chicken stock, etc)
100g sultanas
3 tablespoons coconut milk from a can
lemon juice, to taste
sea salt

Melt the butter in a lidded saucepan with the turmeric. Once melted, add the rice and stir in until the rice is completely coated and starting to turn an opaque colour. Add the stock, sultanas and 1 teaspoon of salt and bring rapidly to the boil.

Reduce the heat to a simmer, place the lid on the pan and cook for 10 minutes (don't peek). The rice should have absorbed all the stock and be tender; if not, replace the lid and continue cooking for another minute or two. If it looks dry, you can always add a little boiling water from the kettle, but I very rarely need to.

Once the liquid has been absorbed and the rice is fluffy, remove from the heat and stir in the coconut milk. You should not need to strain the rice. Season with a little lemon juice and salt, if required, and serve immediately.

Basic Meat Stock

makes 1 litre

Stocks and stock cubes are a nightmare if you are gluten free. I was so overly cautious when Ben was diagnosed that I got into the habit of making my own. I know this is time-consuming, but when I am cooking a roast or while clearing up afterwards, I throw the bones into a stock pot with the veg and simmer them. These are not exact quantities, and if you don't want to use the garlic or celery, perhaps, do leave them out and add different herbs, spices and chillies. Making stock is about using up bits from the fridge and not wasting things, so if you have a broccoli stalk, for example, throw it in the pot.

1 chicken carcass or 450g chicken wings; or 2 beef ribs or oxtails; or 3–4 pork rib bones; or lamb bones from the butcher (neck of lamb is great or shoulder/leg lamb bones)
1 tablespoon sunflower oil
3 large carrots, roughly chopped
3 sticks celery, roughly chopped
2–3 onions or shallots (approx. 250g)
2 bay leaves, fresh if possible
3–4 sprigs of fresh thyme
½ garlic bulb (optional)

Brown off the meat bones in the oil in a large stock pot for around 5 minutes. You will see a lovely golden colour start to appear on the base of the pan; do keep an eye open, and if it starts to look too dark, use a wooden spoon to scrape it off the base and into the pan.

Add all the remaining ingredients and cook for a further 5–10 minutes until a lovely golden crust builds up on the bottom of the pan.

Add about 250ml of water to the pan and use a wooden spoon to deglaze the pan, working around the base and scraping off all the golden bits into the water. The water should turn a lovely gravy colour; take your time at this stage and try to get all the flavour into the pan. Add 1.25 litres of water and simmer over a low heat for at least 1 hour.

Using a ladle, remove any scummy bits from the top of the liquid. Strain through a sieve, but for a really fine stock try using a muslin cloth or J-cloth. Leave it to strain for a few minutes and press down to ensure you get as much flavour as possible. Leave the stock to cool. This can be kept in the fridge, covered, for 48 hours, but I usually freeze it in 500ml bags.

Chicken Gravy

This is the wonderful process of taking stocks and reducing them down to make a proper gravy that we all want over our roast dinners and sausage and mash. Thicken your gravy with a little cornflour if you prefer; it depends what we are eating as to whether I prefer thickened gravy or not.

I have used chicken bones and stock, but just replace these with beef, pork, lamb, venison – whatever works with the meal you're eating. If it's a red meat I would use red wine.

1 chicken carcass or 450g
* chicken wings*
1 tablespoon sunflower oil
3 large carrots, roughly chopped
3 sticks celery, roughly chopped
2 onions or shallots, roughly chopped
* (approx. 250g)*
2 bay leaves, fresh if possible
3–4 sprigs of fresh thyme
½ garlic bulb (optional)
250ml white wine
*1.5 litres **gluten-free** chicken stock*
30g cold butter, cubed

Brown off the chicken carcass or wings in the oil in a large stock pot for around 5 minutes. You will see a lovely golden colour start to appear on the base of the pan; do keep an eye on it, and if it starts to look too dark, use a wooden spoon to scrape it off the base and into the pan.

Add all the remaining ingredients except for the wine, chicken stock and butter. Cook for a further 5–10 minutes, until a golden crust starts to build up on the bottom of the pan.

Pour the wine into the pan and use a wooden spoon to deglaze the pan, working around the base and scraping off all the golden bits. The wine should turn a lovely gravy colour; take your time at this stage and try to get all the flavour into the gravy. Leave to simmer for another 5–10 minutes. Time equals flavour when making stocks and gravy, so when the wine has reduced to about a tablespoon of syrup in the bottom of pan, add the stock.

Simmer for 90 minutes over a low heat until the liquid has reduced by about two-thirds. Using a ladle, remove any scummy bits from the top of the liquid. Pass it through a sieve (or you can use a muslin cloth or J-cloth if you prefer) into a pan. Leave it to strain for a few minutes and press down to ensure you get as much flavour as possible.

Just before you're ready to serve, bring the gravy to almost boiling stage, quickly whisk in the butter and serve immediately.

My Tip
I freeze stock in ziplock bags, laid flat in the freezer, in 500ml quantities; on the labels I write when the stock was made and note any ingredients that will affect flavour, such as chilli. They take up very little room and are always to hand – you can use from frozen, or defrost very quickly when required.

Turmeric, Garlic and **Salt-Crusted Roast Potatoes**

serves 4

Who doesn't love a roast potato? This slight twist on the recipe is lovely served with the Braised Garam Masala Shoulder of Lamb on page 84. Be careful, though, the last time I made these they had nearly all disappeared before we sat down to eat!

450g King Edward (or similar) potatoes, cut up for roasting; I like to make them slightly smaller than regular roasties
2 teaspoons ground turmeric
1 teaspoon sea salt
½ garlic bulb
sunflower oil

Preheat the oven to 180°C/160°C Fan/Gas Mark 4. Bring a large saucepan of water to the boil and parboil the potatoes for 10–12 minutes; you should be able to pierce them easily with a sharp knife to about 0.5cm, with the insides still firm. Drain the potatoes in a colander and then gently toss them around so that the edges become fluffy.

Place the potatoes in a baking tray with enough oil to coat them (this will depend on the size of your pan), sprinkle over the turmeric and salt and turn the potatoes, ensuring all are evenly covered and a golden yellow colour. Add the halved garlic bulb, open side down, baste with a little oil and place in the oven for 1 hour.

After an hour, remove from the oven, turn the potatoes and continue to roast for a further 30 minutes.

Remove the potatoes from the oven. Using the back of a fork, squeeze the roasted garlic out of the skins and toss through the potatoes. Serve immediately while hot and crunchy.

hassle free, gluten free

Savoury Chestnut Purée

serves 6–8

This is lovely with turkey, or any game bird, particularly pheasant. I served it on MasterChef with pheasant and the Pickled Apple with Rosemary (page 23), where it had a great reception.

1 x 180g pack vacuum-packed chestnuts
2 banana shallots, or ½ small onion, chopped
2 garlic cloves, chopped
275ml fresh **gluten-free** chicken stock
2–3 sprigs of fresh thyme
50ml Fino sherry
50g unsalted butter
sea salt and freshly ground black pepper

Put all the ingredients into a saucepan and bring to a simmer for around 30 minutes, until almost all the liquid has gone.

Remove the thyme sprigs and use your stick blender or food processor to blend the mixture to a fine purée. Adjust the seasoning to taste.

My Tip
This purée can be made up to 48 hours in advance and gently reheated when required; however, you may need to add a little more chicken stock to loosen it.

Fresh Horseradish Sauce

makes 250g

I am lucky in that my dad grows fresh horseradish in his garden in London, but I do sometimes buy it from local greengrocers and supermarkets. I find the flavour of fresh horseradish sauce superior to the shop-bought versions, and it is very easy to make. Please be careful when grating as the horseradish is really powerful, and if you take a large sniff you will be coughing and spluttering for a long time!

50g finely grated fresh horseradish (you can adjust this quantity to taste, depending on the strength of the horseradish)
200g crème fraîche
½–1 tablespoon lemon juice
pinch of sea salt

Peel and finely grate the fresh horseradish root into a bowl. Please be careful – this is very strong if inhaled.

Combine with the crème fraiche, lemon juice to taste and salt. Leave for at least 2 hours before using, for the flavours to develop. The sauce will keep in a sealed container in the fridge for up to 72 hours.

hassle free, gluten free

Mum's Easy Onion Sauce

serves 4–6

My favourite roast dinner is my mum's leg of lamb with cauliflower and onion sauce. No one knows where the idea came from – it's probably mum's own creation – but it's delicious, so much so that I did a curried version of it in the final of MasterChef, and that went rather well! This is the basic recipe – it makes a wonderful purée if you cook the onions down further, or add a little gluten-free garam masala for a curried version.

1 large onion, finely chopped
1 bay leaf
350ml milk, plus a little extra for making the cornflour paste
2–3 teaspoons cornflour
sea salt and freshly ground black pepper

Put the onions, bay leaf, milk and a little salt and pepper in a pan over a low heat and simmer slowly for about 20 minutes, until the milk is reduced by half.

Mix the cornflour with a little milk until it is the consistency of double cream.

Pour the cornflour mixture into the pan a little at a time, stirring all the time to make a rich, thick, creamy sauce. Adjust the seasoning to taste – I make mine very peppery.

You can blend the sauce with a stick blender to a smooth consistency, or I just mash it, and serve it in a jug to pour over the meat and veg at the table.

index

218

Coeliac UK is the charity for people who need to live without gluten. They provide independent, trustworthy advice and support, strive for better gluten-free food to be more widely available, and fund crucial research to manage the impacts of gluten and find answers to coeliac disease.

Living a strict lifelong gluten-free diet due to Coeliac disease, or another medical condition, can be challenging. We give our members the resources and support to get on the right track and be able to shop, cook, travel and eat out with confidence.

Helping you understand and manage your symptoms

The charity can help you understand whether your symptoms may be Coeliac disease. Coeliac disease is a serious autoimmune disease where the body's immune system attacks its own tissues when you eat gluten. This causes damage to the lining of the gut and means that the body can't properly absorb nutrients from food. Coeliac disease is not an allergy or food intolerance; the only treatment for Coeliac disease is a strict gluten-free diet for life.

Coeliac disease symptoms

Everyone is different, but if you have Coeliac disease the most common symptoms you can get when you eat gluten are:

- stomach pain
- frequent bouts of diarrhoea or loose stools
- nausea, feeling sick and vomiting
- lots of gas and bloating
- feeling tired all the time, ongoing fatigue
- anaemia (you would be told if you're anaemic following a blood test)
- mouth ulcers
- constipation

There is a skin condition linked to Coeliac disease called Dermatitis Herpetiformis and symptoms include red raised patches on the skin and severe itching and stinging.

If you are experiencing symptoms when eating foods that contain wheat, barley, rye or oats and think you have a sensitivity to gluten, it's important to first rule out Coeliac disease.

Getting diagnosed

If you suffer with any of the symptoms mentioned try Coeliac UK's online assessment at coeliac.org.uk to find out if you should be tested. If the results are positive then you are recommended to speak to your GP for further testing.

It is important that you do not cut gluten out of your diet until you get confirmation of Coeliac disease by your GP, otherwise you may get an inaccurate test result.

Making gluten-free living easier

Switching to a gluten-free diet can feel overwhelming, but the right information can make all the difference. Coeliac UK provides all the tools to eat gluten free, whether you are at home or travelling abroad.

The charity has been instrumental in helping the food industry to embrace the provision of gluten-free food with more confidence and skill. Because of the charity's work, you can eat out here in the UK with a greater degree of confidence, have greater choice when it comes to buying gluten-free products, and purchase more gluten-free products from more places.

Look for their symbols of choice, quality and safety to know your needs are being met.

No life limited by gluten

The charity's vision is a world where no one's life is limited by gluten. That is the vision which drives their research, campaigning and fundraising efforts. You can help them achieve their vision more quickly by joining in and supporting their efforts.

To find out more about Coeliac UK's membership, fundraising and research activities visit coeliac.org.uk

about the author

Since winning MasterChef in 2016, Jane has continued testing herself by working with a number of amazing chefs at their restaurants across the UK including Marcus Wareing, Atul Kochher, Jason Atherton, Michel Roux and Michael O'Hare.

Jane has also presented at numerous food and drink shows around the UK, such as BBC Good Food, Foodies, Ideal Home and many others. Her travels have taken her from Edinburgh to Brighton and everywhere in-between, and on the way she has learnt that she has a love of presenting her recipes and chatting to people about food. Jane has appeared on numerous programmes, including *BBC Breakfast*, *Loose Women* and *Women's Hour*.

First and foremost Jane is still a mum for her four children, cooking everyday for her family, walking the dogs and, this year, attempting to get Ben through his GCSEs. Like most mums, she is busy balancing work and life.

One day a week is put aside for support for charities which are very close to Jane's heart: Coeliac UK, The Ark Cancer Charity, The Haven and others. As well as working with charities, Jane is also working closely with local schools to share her enthusiasm for food amongst the students.

www.janecdevonshire.com

acknowledgements

To my lovely husband Mark and children, Sam, Rebecca, Harry and Ben. My brother Colin for treating me to all those restaurants and constantly obsessing over food with me. And my mum and dad; you are amazing. I love you all lots, thank you.

A huge thank you to my lovely agent Anne, you believed in me and this book from the start, and made it happen.

And to all the wonderful people at Absolute Press who have put so much time and effort into helping this virgin author produce something that she can be so very proud of and looks so beautiful.

Thank you to Phase Eight for the lovely clothes I borrowed for the cover photoshoot.

I want to thank Coeliac UK not only for working with me on this book and checking all my recipes, but also for the invaluable support you offer to people with coeliac disease and others who need to avoid gluten every day. After 12 years coping on our own I signed up to the charity's website, and this has helped Ben and I so very much. The information available and their Food Checker App, which we both use on our phones all the time, is an invaluable tool that is integral to supporting my ability to cook gluten free food for my family.

You can donate or sign up for membership at coeliac.org.uk.

credits

Publisher Jon Croft
Commissioning Editor Meg Boas
Senior Editor Emily North
Art Director and Designer Marie O'Shepherd
Photographer Mike Cooper
Food Stylist Elizabeth Fox
Food Stylist Assistant Cassie Linford
Copyeditor Rachel Malig
Proofreader Margaret Haynes
Indexer Zoe Ross
Cover outfit Phase Eight, phase-eight.com

ABSOLUTE PRESS
Bloomsbury Publishing Plc
50 Bedford Square, London, WC1B 3DP, UK

BLOOMSBURY, ABSOLUTE PRESS and the Absolute Press logo are
trademarks of Bloomsbury Publishing Plc

First published in Great Britain in 2018

A catalogue record for this book is available from the British Library

Library of Congress Cataloguing-in-Publication data has been applied for

ISBN   HB: 978-1-4729-5749-8
        ePDF: 978-1-4729-5748-1
        eBook: 978-1-4729-5750-4

2 4 6 8 10 9 7 5 3 1

Printed and bound in China by C&C Offset Printing Co., Ltd

Bloomsbury Publishing Plc makes every effort to ensure that the papers used
in the manufacture of our books are natural, recyclable products made
from wood grown in well-managed forests. Our manufacturing processes
conform to the environmental regulations of the country of origin.

To find out more about our authors and books visit www.bloomsbury.com
and sign up for our newsletters.